FIVE STONES & A BURNT STICK

Wisdom stories about intimacy

FIVE STONES & A BURNT STICK

Wisdom stories about intimacy

Ernesto Lozada-Uzuriaga Steele

First published in the United States of America 2009 by
Strategic Book Publishing
845 Third Avenue, 6th Floor – 6016
New York, NY 10022

Copyright © 2009
All rights reserved – Ernesto Lozada-Uzuriaga Steele

This paperback edition first published 2014 by
Whispering Tree Original Books
Copyright © 2014
All rights reserved – Ernesto Lozada-Uzuriaga Steele

No part of this book may be reproduced or transmitted in any form or by any means: graphic, electronic, or mechanical; including photocopying, recording, taping, or by any information storage retrieval system; without the permission, in writing, of the publisher.

Whispering Tree Original Books
http://www.whisperingtreeoriginalbooks.com

ISBN: 978-0-9927363-1-6

Published in the United Kingdom

Book Design: M2 Media – Marek Mularczyk – Soul Travel Lodge
Photo cover: Marie Steele & Rachel Thomas

Contents

Prologue		1
I	**The Burning Bush**	5
	The First Stone: *Demarcation*	8
II	**Is It A Dream?**	11
	The Second Stone: *Difference*	17
III	**Welcome Home**	20
	The Third Stone: *Dwelling*	30
IV	**My Brother**	35
	The Fourth Stone: *Disclosure*	46
V	**Father and Son**	54
	The Fifth Stone: *Discovery*	64
VI	**The Last Night**	70
	The Burnt Stick *The Sacred Fire*	84
Epilogue		88
Acknowledgments		91
About The Author		92

"We need creative and readable ways to access profound and personal things. Divine and human intimacy are of one piece, but we are all afraid to go there and few tell us how. Let Ernesto lead you!"
Father Richard Rohr, O.F.M.
Center for Action and Contemplation

"In the tradition of the great myth-makers and storytellers, Ernesto Lozada-Uzuriaga Steele leads us on a joyful and reverent journey into the heart of what it means to be spiritual. For those unhelped by traditional religion, this story will open windows and doors."
Brian McLaren, author and speaker

"This prayerful, imaginative, poetic meditation from the soul of Moses and his wife and daughter is a scripture-soaked immersion in the living Christ who speaks through these words."
Eugene H Peterson, Professor Emeritus of Spiritual Theology
Regent College, Vancouver. Translator of The Message

"We often wonder how the dry bones of scripture can live for today's readers and hearers. Here is one powerful, imaginative, and stimulating approach. In a prosaic age, here is poetry. In a two-dimensional culture, here are three dimensions. In an age where intimacy is made cheap, here is intimacy made wise."
The Right Reverend John Pritchard, Bishop of Oxford

"This bold and imaginative exploration of Moses' hidden moments takes us deep into the divine heart which created us for intimacy. Both a touching love story of husband and wife, and a profound reflection on doubt and discovery, it challenges us to examine our own hearts for reflections of the divine."

Reverend Dr. Mark Harris, Chaplain of Oriel College, Oxford

"This beautiful and profound poetic book, which through Moses and his family celebrates the love between husband and wife, brothers, father and son, father and daughter, and God and man, will reward, enrich, and encourage. Life need not be as bleak as we often make it."

Church Times

Dedication

*You engraved on my wedding ring,
I will inscribe it on this page.*

To my beloved Marie

Prologue

Before Moses, the old prophet of God, moved on into the deeper knowledge of eternal rest, he sent for his daughter Miriam to come to see him one final time. Standing stooped at the entrance to his tent, Moses welcomed her with a trembling voice: "You are growing more beautiful, like your mother."

"Father, you should be resting," Miriam replied, gently kissing her beloved father on his forehead, while she lovingly guided him towards his chair.

"Miriam, I must talk with you," he said, with a certain urgency in his voice.

"What is it, Father?" she enquired with concern.

The old man paused and looked deep into his daughter's eyes. "It is about your inheritance. When I die, in accordance with tradition, your brothers will inherit all my earthly goods. But do not worry. I have made good provision for you and have reserved for you something much more precious than all my material wealth."

"What is it, Father?" Miriam asked, intrigued.

"Five stones and one burnt stick," was Moses' earnest reply.

"Five stones and one burnt stick?" Miriam echoed, in confusion. "But, Father, I don't understand."

Moses paused before responding solemnly, "The five

stones and burnt stick are symbols of the sacred wisdom I received as a blessing when, many years ago, I first met God face-to-face. This wisdom is more precious than gold; it is worth far more than rubies."

"But what is this wisdom, Father?" Miriam asked with growing curiosity.

"It is the wisdom of intimacy," Moses replied quietly. "These symbols represent the five different paths and movements towards intimacy—intimacy with God and intimacy with others."

Miriam sat, stilled by his words and by her own pondering thoughts, waiting for her father to continue.

"This wisdom will guide you in your understanding of the great mystery of all life. It will assist you in unfolding the—" Moses spluttered and his whole body was shaken by a violent spasm of coughing.

"Father, please," Miriam implored. "You are not well. You must try to get some rest."

Ignoring her pleas, Moses continued, fervently now: "God created us to experience intimacy, and be intimate with one another. Hear me when I tell you that intimacy is the entire purpose of our existence—" Moses paused, and then, in a low voice, whispered, "Miriam, it is this which I leave as my inheritance for you."

Concerned and confused, Miriam smiled at her father and gently kissed his forehead once again. "Thank you, Father."

"Stay close, my child," Moses whispered. And then, pouring some pure oil into a wooden bowl, he dipped his aged hands into it and reverently anointed Miriam, first on her forehead and then on the palms of her hands. He then blessed her, solemnly declaring: "Miriam, I leave in your charge this hessian bag containing five stones and one

PROLOGUE

burnt stick. They are symbols of the divine wisdom of intimacy. Use them to guide all women towards the attainment of true intimacy—with God and with all His children. And, when the time is right, you will be called to teach and share this wisdom with those men who are ready to listen and learn. These five stones and the burnt stick will be passed from woman to woman until the perfect day comes when their wisdom will be shared by the whole of humanity."

As Moses spoke, a northerly wind gathered strength, blowing around the tent, extinguishing the candles, and replacing their light with beautiful dancing ever-lengthening and deepening shadows. As Miriam watched their dance play across her father's face, Moses breathed his last breath, and she suddenly sensed that his sacred soul had become one with that sacred wind. A holy Presence filled the tent and Miriam experienced the profound peace of perfect love.

***

Throughout history, from generation to generation, using ceremonial dance and ritual celebration (whether it is within the oral tradition or in written form), faithful women have preserved the ancient truth and sacred wisdom of intimacy, using these symbols of five stones and a burnt stick. Remarkably, this wisdom has survived and traveled across time, religion, race, and culture. And now is come the age for all humanity to learn the sacred truth that will guide us all towards the mystery of intimacy–intimacy with God and intimacy with others. Today is the day. Today brothers and sisters, this sacred Wisdom will be passed on to you.

I
The Burning Bush

It was a clear night, like many other nights in that desert wilderness. Vast and strewn with countless stars, the sky above Mount Horeb was alight with brightness and though he meant to be looking after his father-in-law's flock, he scoured the heavens, seeking a sign, a star, or some other omen to give answers to the longing of his heart. Yet that night, too, the sky was silent, the stars sharing none of their mystery. His soul groaned within him, while his voice hurled this cry towards the stars' muteness: "Here I stand, an old and broken man, a runaway, a fugitive, lost and rootless in a foreign land."

And then, overwhelmed by sadness, he buried his face in his hands and wept loud and bitter tears.

It was then that it came. At first, it was just a sound. The north Wind howled, as often it did, yet now it seemed to carry snatched whispers of some distant conversation. The flock picked up the sound, while Horeb itself seemed to hold its breath and the whole mountain grew still, as if in wondering premonition of events beyond its ken. Alert now, the old shepherd lifted his head, straining to hear, sensing the presence of something or, perhaps, someone. The dangers were many on Horeb and, fearing for his flock, he stood, his staff clasped to him, and began to move slowly through his sheep. Nothing. He heard nothing. "Nothing is amiss," he reassured himself, relieved. But suddenly, far beyond the flock, he glimpsed a strange light. Placing himself between his flock and whatever lay ahead, he moved fearfully and cautiously forward. Before him lay what appeared to be a fire burning bright in the darkness.

"But who could have started this fire?" he asked himself, his heart hammering against his chest. "Is anyone there?" he shouted into the night. Silence. No response. All was still. He paused momentarily and then continued, as if drawn towards the fire, its heat and light now casting their strange warmth on his own face as he approached. And then, again, he stopped transfixed, for the fire which came from within the bush was refining all around it with its brightness, and yet the bush itself was not consumed. And so he stood silent and pondering before the sight. In that silent wonder, he sensed from deep within the bush a voice calling his name. And deep within his own heart, he felt the words forming and then rising to his lips, and he heard himself replying, "Here I am."

That night on Horeb the old shepherd realized why this place was called the Mount of God, for it was there that he, himself, first encountered Yahweh, the God of his fathers, the Hebrew God so unlike the gods of Egypt. And from that encounter, in a circle of blazing light, he began to fathom the strange destiny which had drawn him to the Hebrew people, and to realize that the passions and fragments of his life were purposed, and that who he was had always been recognized and realized before his God. That night the old shepherd realized that he was known and loved, and that God had called him as Prophet, Leader and Liberator of His people in Israel. And that night, in this Holy Presence, he was given the wisdom of life and grasped the purpose of our existence as a people. God's words reverberated through him:

"We have been created for intimacy: intimacy with God and intimacy with others."

He went back to his flock, but his heart was now alight with this newfound divine knowledge and wisdom. He lay down but couldn't sleep, euphoric before the sights and sounds that blazed in the eyes of his heart. In his mind he rehearsed the miracles that had illuminated his night and, restless at the thought of them, he stepped outside his tent into the night to fill his lungs and clear his mind to better ponder its meaning. As he had done so many lonely nights here in the desert, the shepherd sat down on a rock and lifted his eyes towards the heavens. But now, instead of silence, he sensed purpose; instead of loneliness, Presence; and though he still had questions and sensed his old enemy, self-doubt, he somehow for the first time in his life knew that he had a place in the cosmic order, and that somehow Yahweh meant to write his life into His divine salvation story.

The First Stone:
Demarcation

I heard a voice calling my name: "Moses! Moses!" And so I drew closer to discover who it was that called me. My eyes were immediately drawn to a bush, blazing with such intensity that a sense of awe permeated my whole heart. Suddenly, from within that bush, the voice came again.

"Do not come any closer!" I stopped immediately.

"Do not come any closer!" the voice repeated. "Stay standing where you are."

"Who is this voice that knows my name?" I wondered to myself. "Is it an angel? Is it a god?" There was no way to know, and as I marvelled, I realized I was too terrified to ask any questions. I knew only that I could do nothing but wait. Then ... suddenly ... the voice commanded me: "Take a stick from the ground and draw a circle around yourself." I obeyed immediately, stunned by the overwhelming Presence, by the intense heat and by the voice that knew my name. Using a burnt stick, I knelt down and drew a circle in the earth around me.

"That circle is your space," the voice said. "It is your sacred space."

"What is my sacred space?" I managed to ask,

THE FIRST STONE: *DEMARCATION*

trembling.

"That sacred space is you," the voice replied.

"But what is me? Who am I? I have been seeking this answer for years, and yet I remain lost and confused."

"I created you, Moses. You are a sacred being, a mystery that words cannot yet explain. What and who you are is something that you will discover only as you travel the pathways of intimacy. It is only through being intimate with me and with others that you will learn who you truly are."

"Show me the path of intimacy," I begged the voice. "I want to learn."

"The first thing to learn about the mystery of intimacy is the importance of recognizing and marking out the boundaries of your sacred space. The circle in which you are standing rep-resents those boundaries." The voice resonated in my spirit and through my very being, and then continued:

"The mystery of intimacy is to draw near to the other person whilst firmly holding and living within the boundaries that contain your own sacred space. If you abandon the boundaries containing your sacred space, you will destroy the possibility of any true intimacy. The boundaries of your sacred space will guide you and help you to honour and respect the sacred space and the integrity of the other. Without this respect for yourself and others, intimacy becomes a form of domination, oppression, and violation of the other. It becomes a means to control the other and to impose one's own will upon that of others. It will become pure evil. The path of intimacy acknowledges the freedom of the other, their free will, and their right and responsibility to choose. The path of intimacy respects the integrity of the other; it never invades or abuses the sacred space of the other.

"It is important that you protect the boundaries of your sacred space, not from fear or hostility —which I will tell you more of later—but for your own protection and the fulfilment of your own unique divine mystery. All human beings need this. Inside you and others there are unknown forces which need to be contained by the boundaries until personal recognition of them comes, and you learn how to understand and deal with them. In you and others are secrets that must remain concealed until the time is right for them to be revealed. Within you and others, ghosts reside who need to rest and be kept at bay. Your boundaries will protect you and others from forces which are sometimes beyond control and understanding. Your boundaries will change, grow and expand as you travel further along the path of intimacy, but, Moses, they will never disappear.

"Moses, the path of intimacy demands that we draw clear boundaries. These boundaries are born of respect and love—not fear, selfishness or mistrust—and serve to preserve the soul, body, mind, and heart of you and others. Demarcation is not a barrier separating you from others, but a gate that opens and closes, welcoming and bidding farewell to those who enter into your sacred space. Boundaries are signs of mutual respect. The path towards the mystery of intimacy demands that you draw clear boundaries. The path of intimacy begins with demarcation.

"You are there in the circle. I am here in the burning bush. We have both made it clear where we stand. We both know where our sacred space and boundaries lie. I will respect your boundaries and I will respect your sense of being. In doing this, we will travel the path of intimacy together and you will learn to do the same with others."

II

Is It A Dream?

He was awakened by a kiss. It was not, however, the tender kiss of Zipporah, his wife, but that of a small lamb who had sheltered in his tent from the piercing chill of the night before. Today was a new day. The sun had already risen and flooded the tent. Its light bathed and warmed his cold, sweat-drenched body, which was still trembling with thoughts of what had occurred the night before. Moses felt shocked and stunned by the immense responsibility which the Sacred one had entrusted to him. Fear gripped his soul and filled his entire being.

"It cannot be possible. It cannot be me ... If I return to Egypt they will kill me." Hearing the fear in his own voice brought the faces of Zipporah, his wife, and Gerson, their only son, to his mind. "I cannot leave my family. They are the most precious people in my world and my entire reason for living."

He had wanted a change in his life. He had looked to the stars for new omens, and he had wanted a purpose—beyond the responsibility for his wife and son—to give meaning to his existence. But he had never expected this present painful dilemma to be set before him. His heart felt torn in two—thinking first of his loved ones here, and then of those suffering people whose voices now called to him from Egypt. More than anything else, at this moment, he felt a sickening, desperate terror at the thought of leaving his beloved wife and son. "Zipporah and I are very different. We have contrasting cultures and come from opposite backgrounds. Whilst I have known privilege and wealth, Zipporah has known only scarceness and hardship. As a child I was brought up in Pharaoh's palace, in one of the greatest cities in the world, surrounded by obliging servants, magnificent buildings and pyramids. Zipporah, however, grew up in the desert, surrounded by hills, her father's flocks, wild animals and tall palm trees. Whilst I learned the arts of politics, war and science from the best scholars in the kingdom, Zipporah, taught by her mother and the other tribeswomen, studied the properties and virtues of every wild desert plant, learned the name of every stone, observed the moods of the clouds and learned to interpret the bleating of the flocks. As people, we are very different in essence. Whilst Zipporah can always read and know the hearts of others, I discern the thoughts and minds of my enemies. Zipporah is devoutly spiritual. She has rituals for every occasion and prayers for every event. Her God is one who gives her strength and purpose, and guides her in all aspects of her daily living. I have seen her carefully select stones from the desert floor and use them to design serpent-shaped pathways in the sand. I have watched as she has silently retraced the path of her sunlit labyrinths, praying to and loving her God. Her spirit renewed, she finds her calm and, in loving her, I have grown to admire and respect her and her ways. But I myself mistrust religion and consider it utter superstition. Zipporah and I are very different; nevertheless, we met and fell in love and our love has grown and blossomed like a flower in rich, sun-kissed

IS IT A DREAM?

earth, and today that love is stronger than ever it has ever been." Moses was comforted by these thoughts which distracted him for a moment, as did the lambs which played and frolicked before him. But disturbing, fearful thoughts almost immediately interrupted his reverie.

"How can I tell Zipporah that God has told me to return to Egypt in order to liberate my people? It is madness! She will never believe that God has asked me to undertake such a fear-some task." Moses looked up at the sky, anxiously seeking an answer, his breath short and rasping and his heart beating loudly in his ears. "Zipporah will never believe what I have to say. She will laugh at me and think that the solitude of the hills and the heat of the sun have disturbed my mind and reason."

Suddenly, Moses was seized by a powerful anger and resentment towards the one who had presented him with such an impossible task, who had charged him with such a terrible responsibility. "There is no end to this dilemma. If Zipporah does believe me and agrees to let me go, I know that she will make herself ill with worry, and the dread that she may never see me again." These thoughts terrified Moses and left him feeling desolate and terribly alone.

"If I were to leave for Egypt, it would break her heart. We have planned to have another child. 'It is time,' she told me before I left her to come for this season with the flocks to Horeb. 'It is time.' I agreed with her, delighted by the thought. Time passes quickly. The summer of our love has nearly passed, and we are beginning our journey towards autumn and uncertain winter. If we are to have another child, now is the time. If I go to Egypt, we may never have that time." Moses was overcome with grief even by the thought of this.

"Maybe it was all a dream," Moses thought in desperate

denial. But he knew that it was not a dream, and that his heart, soul, and body were still alive with the blazing Presence he had heard from within the burning bush the night before. "I can only wish that it was … just a dream," he lamented. "One man and his brother against the mighty Pharaoh? It is madness. I would never return home alive to my beloved wife and son."

Moses paced back and forth through his flock, occasionally touching a head or back, vaguely, vainly searching for some tangible reassurance and guidance. "Maybe I should return to the place where I encountered the Holy one, and reason with him. I could explain that I am the wrong person to save my people from Pharaoh's oppression, that I cannot return to Egypt, and that I need and want to be with my family and care for them. Maybe then the Holy one will release me from this commission and choose someone else, someone younger, someone unencumbered by the past and by family commitments, someone who would not fail Him."

With a sudden surge of hope, Moses gathered his flock and retraced his steps towards the place where he had first caught sight of the burning bush the night before. But hope died the instant he saw the mocking remains, the grey ash of last night's burning bush.

"Other than the knowledge that burns within me, these ashes are the only testament to what was between us, the only witness to the covenant we have made, and to the commitment I made and must now honour." Moses slumped down onto a rock and wept tears of fear, grief and resignation.

"Why me? Why me?" His broken cry punctuated gut-wrenching sobs. He was answered only by a still and deep silence. "Where are you? Talk to me! Talk to me, I beg of

IS IT A DREAM?

you. I have so much that I need to say. I am desperate. I cannot do what you want me to. I am terrified. How can you ask me to leave all that I love and return to the place that I vowed I had left behind me forever? How? I do not understand why you have asked this of me." Again, he was answered only by the still and deep silence. Moses sobbed until he had no more tears, and his exhausted body ached from crying.

Then, without warning, a mighty wind gathered strength and raged around him, threatening to destroy or clear everything from its path. Fearing for his very life, Moses crouched behind—then clung to—the rock on which he had previously rested. Through gritted eyes he watched as a hot wind tore through the landscape, tossing boulders, stripping leaves and branches from some trees, and uprooting others that hindered its progress through the land. At last the wind grew calmer, and a gentle breeze moved towards Moses. He felt a gentle, cooling breeze on his face, and in the breeze came the sounds of a gentle silence. Deep within him he heard, whispered, the message: "I will be with you! I will be with you!"

A sense of profound peace stilled him and everything around him. For the first time since encountering the burning bush, Moses experienced true serenity and strength. Moses knew he was once again in the presence of the Holy one. Without thinking, he fell to his knees and kissed the ground. "This is a holy place," he said with a quiet, yet joyful reverence.

In the strength of this revelation, and guided as if by an unseen hand, Moses then picked up five stones and a burnt stick which he found lying at his feet. He placed them carefully in the hessian bag he wore at his waist, and then stood to see to his flock. Strangely, in the stillness, he realized that the flock had not been disturbed by the storm. Their heads rose only when they heard the sound of his voice. And so, with renewed strength and purpose, Moses led the flock back down to where he had put up his tent. And with his charges safe and near, he sought shelter from the sun, took the first stone out of his bag, and began to carve into it the words of wisdom, understanding and knowledge that he had been blessed by the Holy one to receive into his being.

The Second Stone:
Difference

"Take off your sandals, for the place where you are standing is holy ground!" The voice came from within the burning bush. Without hesitation, Moses knelt down to remove his sandals and then rose again, his head bowed, to stand within the circle which the Holy one had previously instructed him to draw around him on the ground.

After a pause, the Holy one spoke. "Moses, my child, I want you to know that we are different. I am the Holy one. I am begotten, not made. I am the creator of heaven and earth. I lovingly created you in my own image. You are a man, a human being, and I am the eternal God. We are different: like day and night, air and fire, earth and water, good and evil, man and woman. We are different. My thoughts are not your thoughts. My ways are not your ways. We are different. Moses, we will never be the same. We are forever different." on hearing these words, Moses felt a sadness and longing in his heart.

"Why are you sad?" asked the voice of the Holy one.

"I feel sad because we are different, and I fear that this difference will keep us apart forever. I want you to know you and understand you. I want to understand this ..."

Moses' voice trailed off, and again there was silence between them.

"Do not be sad, Moses. Your worry and sadness are unfounded. It is in knowing that you are different that you will begin to travel your journey on the path of intimacy," replied the Sacred other with deep knowing and love.

"But how can we have intimacy if we are different?" Moses asked, confused.

"In order to experience the mystery of intimacy, you must first recognize that all people are different, unique, and special. You will never be the same as anyone else. You must embrace this truth as a sacred wisdom, and know that it is to be cherished, respected, and celebrated."

"I do not understand," Moses replied, searchingly.

"My beautiful son, the wisdom of intimacy teaches that we must not need the other person to be like, to speak like, to think like, to feel like and to dream like ourselves. The path of intimacy embraces and nurtures the difference between yourself and the other. It respects and nourishes this uniqueness and difference. The path of intimacy creates a space in which the other is encouraged and enabled to find their own path, be their own self, think their own thoughts, speak with their own voice, acknowledge their own feelings, and dream their own dream. Intimacy celebrates the difference between the self and the other. The richness of your differences will always surprise, delight, challenge, and teach you. These differences will never be exhausted in the brevity of life. Every day will be one of great discovery and wonder. In becoming more intimate, you continue to affirm the differences between yourselves. To recognize and respect the difference of the other is the first essential step on the mysterious path of intimacy."

THE SECOND STONE: *DIFFERENCE*

Moses listened with quiet attentiveness, trying to relate this wisdom to his own life experience.

"Moses, difference is not an obstacle but a gift to those who seek and know intimacy. If you are willing, and have the courage, intimacy with me your God or with any of my other children is possible. Do not be afraid of one who is different from you. Know, instead, that it is this difference between you that will enable true intimacy to flourish. Indeed, Moses, can you not see that this has been so with you and your beloved wife Zipporah?"

Moses nodded in agreement and in growing awareness that this encounter with God and the challenge to return to Egypt, like all the days of his life, had been written into the book of God.

III

Welcome Home

"I will see him today," she repeated to herself almost incessantly, the smile in her voice shining from her face as well. "I will be with him tonight," she whispered with joyous expectation, knowing that from the moment he had left, her entire being had been longing for his homecoming.

It has been a long absence. It was forty days since he had left with the flock to search for green pastures in the isolated hills of Mount Horeb. And through those forty days it was he who had occupied her thoughts both day and night. He had lived in her dreams and slept in her womb; he had lived in her heart, in her memory, and in her every waking moment, too. On every occasion and in every conversation, his name waited playfully about the corners of her mouth and rose and fell within her with each breath she took. She prayed constantly to the Creator of All Things that He would protect her beloved from the wild animals, the bandits, and the dangers of the night, and that He would return him safely to her.

"At times it is almost unbearable," she sighed sadly and wearily to herself. "Nothing is the same when he goes away, nothing. Without him, everything in heaven and earth seems strangely still, as if all creation were waiting with me for his return. Without him, my soul hungers and thirsts for his sustaining love. Without him my life—in all its dimensions and senses—feels parched and barren."

Zipporah walked slowly and ceremoniously along her newly laid, winding labyrinth of glowing white pebbles. With each step her thoughts grew calmer and slower, until they and she merged into a trusting restfulness of quiet knowing and being. Still and peaceful, she stood at the labyrinth's end and spoke quietly to the wind, which gently brushed her face and hair.

"Whilst I know that times such as these, apart from my beloved husband, are painful and torturous, I also know that the lessons taught to me, as a result of this experience, are both deep and fruitful. In his absence I have thought and understood more of the secrets of his heart, and listened to the wisdom of my own soul and learned more of the language of love."

The wind heard and comforted Zipporah, and then wrapped these wise words in the folds of its cloak and carried them away. A messenger of the Holy one, the wind knew that these words needed to be saved and pondered and delivered to another time, another place and another people.

Later that day, while talking with a faithful servant, Zipporah remembered again the dream she had dreamt. "In my dream I saw a blazing fire residing in my beloved's heart. It was a sacred fire, an eternal fire from God, a fire which teaches, transforms, cleanses, and heals everything. Maybe," she reflected, "it is a good omen." And then, as she had throughout this day, her entire being smiled as she whispered: "My beloved returns home to me today." In his return home to her, it was as if Moses were enabling

FIVE STONES AND A BURNT STICK

Zipporah to again return home fully to herself.

The day was passing and the sun was setting, transforming the sky with a spectacular blaze of colour. And yet there was still no sight of him. Zipporah grew agitated and anxious. "It is unusual for Moses to return home so late. I fear that something may have happened to him." Then, fretfully, she said to a servant, "Where could he be?" Not waiting for a reply, she began silently to fear that bandits or wild animals might have harmed him.

The sun finally slipped below the horizon. A chill breeze descended from the high hills, and figures of dust began to rise up in their dance around the desert dunes. All was silent. But then, suddenly, she heard the long, deep bellow of a ram's horn: the signal that someone was approaching the desert camp. "It must be him!" she cried with tears of relief and joy, her heart beating loudly in her chest. Zipporah raised her eyes, arms, and heart to God, and gave Him thanks for answering her prayers and returning her beloved home safely to her. Her eyes darted towards the mirror her mother had given them on their wedding day. Zipporah wanted to look her most beautiful for the return of her beloved. Reassured, she ran outside the tents to wait with their son, their servants, and their servants' children for the long-awaited arrival of her husband. Her eyes scanned the horizon, but she could see nothing. Her stomach churned with fear and her breath grew quicker and shallow. "Perhaps it is a false alarm. Perhaps the desert has played some cruel trick on the eyes of the watchman."

As she looked through the billowing curtain of blowing sand, she turned to her servants and asked in longing and desperation, "Where is he?" Suddenly, one of the young servants discerned a stooped figure slowly moving towards them through the lengthening shadows.

WELCOME HOME

"Over there! Over there!" she cried.

Zipporah looked eagerly to where the servant was pointing and almost screamed with joy, "It is him!"

She could wait no longer. Gathering up her skirts, she ran towards her husband as fast as she could. Their eyes met first. Both hearts quickened as relief and longing, joy and hope, came surging up from within them. And once in each other's arms, they clung to one another and kissed with passionate urgency, their need and desire to be at one with each other manifest in every limb.

At long last, the wait was over. They were at one, together again in the familiar warmth and presence of the other, and the familiar sense and smell of the other.

"Welcome home, dear husband," Zipporah whispered.

"It is so good to be home," came his exhausted, but grateful reply.

Zipporah drew back from his embrace and studied her husband's face. Moses looked thin and drained. Both his hair and beard had grown long and unkempt, and his skin and clothes were caked with the dust of the desert. "You smell like your own flock!" she laughed playfully.

Moses smiled, looked deep into her eyes and, with a heart full of love, drew her close to him once more. Zipporah laid her head on her husband's chest and heard and felt the strong beating of his heart resound through her own body. Without stirring, she rested and realized that his mind, heart and soul were troubled. Her intuition never failed her. His eyes, his bearing, his whole being told her that Moses was burdened and troubled by something, but by what she did not know. "I will let him talk in his own time," she thought.

Watching their reunion from the tents, all the other women in the camp roared in the traditional way, whilst the men clapped and chanted his name. Moses looked over to his trusted, faithful servants, smiled, and then beckoned to them with open arms. They ran as one to him and embraced him in welcome, sharing the joy at his safe return. Then, all turned together back towards the camp, and Zipporah turned her mind and heart towards seeing to his immediate needs. She asked a servant to prepare a bath for Moses, and another to get food.

"I am not hungry," Moses whispered. "Just tired." And his worn, pale face stopped her insisting.

"There is something wrong," Zipporah thought with concern. "Moses is always hungry on his return. What can I do to help him? He is so obviously troubled by something."

The servants filled the deep terracotta bath with hot water and an assortment of aromatic herbs. Zipporah tested the water to make sure that it was the temperature Moses liked. "Thank you for all that you have done. You can go now," she smiled to the servants. Zipporah wanted to be alone with her husband. She drew the tent's outer flaps together and quietly lit candles near the place where the bath stood. She then began slowly to remove the layered clothing of his desert wanderings. On another night she might have undressed too, joining him in the water. But not tonight. Tonight she wanted first to know him again with her eyes, to feel and be in his presence, and to hear the strong rhythm of his heart. Then, before he caressed her, before they shared in the feast of their bodies and souls, they would already be one. But looking at him, Zipporah realized that tonight was not that sort of night. She knew that tonight the soul of her beloved was troubled and burdened by something that he would struggle to express. "Tonight he seems too tired. He is lost for wounds and bound by that which burdens his heart and soul. But what can it be that disturbs him so?"

Slowly, silently, she began to soap and bathe his whole body: his broad shoulders, his chest, his strong arms and calloused hands, his long legs and his poor feet, which were cut and bruised by his travels. Then—still silently—she began to wash and rinse his hair and beard, teasing out the knotted grass and tangles, and working the scented oils into his scalp and hair to nourish and soften it again. Zipporah did this in loving silence, waiting for him to speak ... if he would. But Moses said nothing. She tried to sing, but her voice grew faint in her throat, and so Zipporah retreated into the silence of her own thoughts and the joy of simply being with him. She held out her hands as he stepped from the bath and then dried her husband's body, anointing his skin with perfumed oil and kneading healing, aromatic balms into his shoulders, hands and feet.

Since his return, only a few words had passed between them. Zipporah was uneasy, and longed to share and try to assuage whatever it was that so disturbed and troubled her husband. "I feel that he is trying to find the words, searching for the right moment to open his heart to tell me what is troubling him," she assured herself. But nothing broke the silence between them.

Moses eased his body onto their bed, his eyes watching every gesture, every move she made. She felt his eyes upon her, and—suddenly feeling shy—she undressed very slowly, slightly unsure of herself and him. Although she had rehearsed this moment many times in her mind, she now found herself searching through her things, trying to find a garment that would please him. At last, finding the white linen nightdress she knew he preferred, Zipporah slipped it over her head and let it slide over her body.

"I am too tired to sleep," he blurted out, breaking the

awkwardness of their silence.

He then struggled to say something else, but Zipporah gently placed her finger on his lips, looked deep into his eyes and, with pure love, gently reassured him, "No, my Beloved. No words tonight." knowing her husband as she did, Zipporah sensed that tonight Moses needed to quietly and simply to lie alongside her once again. And, she reassured herself, sensing that the words her husband needed to speak were not yet ready to be formed.

She gradually dimmed the light around them, extinguishing the candles and allowing the moonlight to take their place, casting a soft light and quickening the clouds' shadows cross his face. All was stillness, save for a distant melody carried to them on a breeze. "Do you hear the music?" she asked Moses in delight.

"Yes!" he replied, smiling, his ears awakening to the music and grateful to the wind.

"One of the servants must be serenading a girl," Zipporah whispered. "Just listen."

They lay together listening quietly, content with the presence of their love for one another and with the music of another couple's love for one another. Slowly, as if enchanted, Zipporah stood and began to sway gently, and then to dance to the music's rhythm.

Moses watched as she gradually abandoned herself to the music. She moved freely and unselfconsciously, with a grace and beauty, passion, ease, and spontaneity unlike anything he had ever seen. Her gestures were both strong and, at the same time, infinitely delicate. Every shape, every whirling turn, every agile leap, and every motion she made seemed to embody and express both the joy and the pain of life. "Zipporah's movements are mysterious," Moses thought, then, suddenly: "Zipporah's dance is like that of an angel with broken wings!"

Her dance filled the tent with beauty, love, freedom, sensuality and dazzling exoticism. Zipporah danced as God danced on each of the seven days of creation, as nature dances when life is born, and as people dance when they dwell safely in God's holy presence. As she danced, the whole creation danced with her. Heaven and earth, the hills and the dunes, the sun and the moon, the stars and the wind, the trees and the birds danced with her joy.

As she danced, Zipporah felt as if her soul and body were truly at one with each other. Through this dance Zipporah's entire being was freed and she knew the sacredness of being at one. Through this dance Zipporah expressed her gratitude and joy in life and in love and felt her inner conflicts resolved, her fears and desire appeased, the secrets of her soul unfolding as she praised the Lord and Creator of All. Within this dance Zipporah discovered the wordless language of the loving heart, and knew intuitively that this was the language of God.

The distant music had stopped long before, but still her body and soul danced. They danced as if they would never stop dancing. Suddenly she realized that she no longer wanted to dance without Moses, and she looked across to her husband, who was watching, captivated by her and the beauty of the dance. Every fibre of her being called to him, and he felt himself rise to meet her. Wordlessly, he joined her, returned her smile and the look that saw deep into his own heart and soul and, drawing her to him, kissed her gently on the forehead. As one they moved to the music of their hearts and the love between them, breathing each other's breath, attuned to every nuance and essential essence of the other. In this dance they knew that they had found one another in a new and different way and that they were communicating in a new language, free of spoken words.

As they danced, Moses found that he was no longer tired and Zipporah found that she was no longer anxious. Together they danced and wordlessly shared what was deep in their hearts and in their souls. The spoken word had become unnecessary, a foreign, cumbersome, redundant, and limiting thing. So concordant were they that Moses was able freely and openly to express all that before had so burdened him and Zipporah listened with unhesitating trust.

"I am saying things that I could not speak of before," Moses marvelled.

"We are revealing ourselves to one another in language unknown to us before," she wondered in awe.

In the voiceless dialogue of dance, they were united. Joined together, through this dance, Moses and Zipporah seemed to exist in another time and in another place. It was, they sensed, a holy place: a place where spiritual beings meet and exist in harmony and love, a place where God dwells and where His being first created the music that illumines the dance of intimacy. That night Moses and Zipporah truly found their home with—and in—each other. That night they learned the language which enabled them at last to truly "welcome home" the other.

The moon and the night merged into one; the music and the silence merged as one and their bodies, too, merged into one, forming a single figure which slowly melted into the shadows of the tent, now filled with the rich scent of their union.

At dawn Zipporah woke and stretched a loving hand out towards her husband's place, only to find that Moses was already up. Sleepy still, her eyes searched the tent and discovered him at its entrance, silhouetted by the light of the new day. In his hand he held a small stone which he seemed to be carving, she knew not why. But Moses was safe, and well, and with her, and with a grateful smile, Zipporah turned back to their bed and fell once more into a peaceful sleep.

The Third Stone:
Dwelling

The fire and blaze did not cease. The burning bush still blistered with great heat and light. I remained standing in my place within the circle, which I had drawn on the ground, pondering all that the Sacred one had told me.

"You will dwell in my presence and share intimacy with me. You will be my prophet," the Holy one said to me. "It is you whom I have chosen to liberate my people. It is you whom I have chosen to be my messenger to the most powerful ruler on earth." I heard these words and fear and a deep sense of all my limitations thrust through my body. I expressed my doubts and fears to Him.

"But I am not eloquent or gifted in the spoken word. I am slow of speech and tongue. How can I be a prophet, and how can I share intimacy with you?"

"You place too much trust and importance in the spoken word," was the Sacred one's response to my despairing question. "Do you really believe that human language can comprehend and express the unfolding mysteries of life or the secrets of your own heart? Do you really believe that it is the spoken word that will make you a prophet, Moses?"

And then, almost like thunder, He challenged me with

this question: "How can the spoken word explain who I am? Moses, do not allow yourself to be misled. Whilst the spoken word has its value, it also has its limitations. The spoken word can only provide glimpses of reality, only glimpses. Although language is necessary for living in community, it does not—it cannot—represent and express everything. There are many matters in this world and in your own heart and soul that are beyond the power and the limitations of the spoken word and formal language."

A deep silence followed, and within it a thousand thoughts and questions rose noiselessly within me. Finally, I managed to say, "But, Holy one, without using words to speak to You, how will I understand and be intimate with You?"

"Moses," replied the Sacred one. "You do not need to understand me. You just need to love and trust me and dwell in my presence. If you are able to do this, you will learn who I am. You will learn the mysteries of my heart and share true intimacy with me."

"But how are we to share intimacy without spoken words?" I countered apprehensively. "Surely we need spoken words in order to express our needs and desires, to share our dreams and have intimacy. Surely, if we are to enjoy intimacy, we need to talk."

"Moses," the Holy one replied firmly. "The more you talk, the less you understand. Intimacy does not depend on the spoken word, but on learning the language of the heart and dwelling in the presence of one another. I will teach you a new language, one that is already hidden in your heart."

"A new language?" I repeated, intrigued.

"Yes, a new language. Now, stand up. I want you to dance."

"I do not understand," I thought to myself. "He said that He would teach me a new language and now He is asking me to dance. It is ridiculous. I cannot dance and I do not want to embarrass and make a fool of myself. I am not going to do it! I cannot do it!"

"You must do as I say," the Sacred one repeated solemnly.

"But Sacred one! I am a man. Since the beginning of creation, the tradition has been for women to dance and for men to watch."

"Moses, trust in me and dance."

"But Sacred one, I cannot! I am a man and I do not know how to dance," I cried anxiously.

"Moses, you can. Believe me. Just trust. Loosen your body. Stop thinking and questioning. Free your fearful self. Welcome your dance, and move," the Sacred one persisted.

"But Sacred one, there is no music. Surely I need music if I am to dance."

"Be quiet and listen to the Silence; then you will hear the music of which you speak."

"I just do not understand," I cried uncomprehendingly.

"Moses, there is always music hiding in the Silence," the Holy one insisted.

Obeying the Sacred one, I closed my eyes and tried in vain to hear the music within the silence. All I could hear was the sound of the wind, but I did not give up. Instead, I listened deeper ... harder ... and gradually I began to discern in the silence a beautiful and lyrical melody. And ... suddenly ... without my knowing ... my body began to move to the rhythm of the melody. "I am dancing!" I cried out in disbelief. "I am dancing like I did as a very young boy. I remember now. I used to dance, secretly, in one of the royal chambers. I do not remember why and when I stopped. Probably when somebody told me that, since the beginning of all creation, it is only women who dance and men who watch."

As I dance, my body moving freely and without inhibition, I feel a miracle taking place within me. My body and soul seem to merge and become the voice of my heart. I find myself "dancing" the things that I could not say before, recognizing and expressing the many feelings and emotions that I have ignored or forgotten for so long. I realize that I am no longer relying on the spoken word, a language limited in its explanation of our temporal reality and conscious world. I realize that I am expressing myself through a language that has cosmic proportions, that I am expressing myself by dancing the language of the heart.

"Moses," said the Sacred one. "Know now that you are speaking the language of the heart—the language of intimacy. The language of spoken words is the language of human ideas and of earthly endeavour. But the language of the heart is God's language. It is the language that connects you with other souls and with the entire cosmos. It is the language you use when your soul and body are in communion. Through dance your soul and your body become one. In giving yourself to the dance, the language of the heart is born within you. This, Moses, is the language of intimacy. This is the exquisite language you speak when you dwell in the presence of the one whom you love. As you learn to speak the language of the heart, you will grow in your awareness of all that is both visible and invisible. As you learn to listen to the language of the heart, you will learn to recognize truly the voice of the one who calls you 'my beloved.'"

As I listened with an open heart to the words of wisdom which were, I knew, transforming my life forever, I continued to dance. In my dance I felt euphorically that I was no longer dancing alone but in the company and presence of the Creator, and that all His creation was dancing with me.

I am not eloquent or wise, but I know that on that night I discovered something of unique profundity. I learned that when my body and soul are united in dance, I can speak and listen to the language of the heart, the language of intimacy, a language which is, ultimately, the language of God. I learned that the more I speak and understand the language of the heart, the more my presence will have the authority to bless and heal, to curse and condemn, and to bind and release all things here on earth, as in heaven. The more I listen to the language of the heart, the more I realize that I can hear the words of God's heart, the steady rhythm of His breath, the music of His Silence. The more I listen to, and speak, the language of the heart, the more I dwell with Him, and know His warm and infinitely loving presence, and know that I am truly intimate with the Sacred one. He has taught me the language of intimacy, and now asks me to be with Him as I live it.

IV

My Brother

The sun dazzles with its brilliance, but Moses is unflinching in his gaze. Two flies noisily pursue one another around him, but Moses' posture remains unchanged. From neighbouring tents the sound of human voices and the bawl of animals trouble the tranquillity of the day, but do not intrude upon his reflections. His eyes are fixed, unswervingly, on the vast horizon of silence and swirling sand. Moses sits strong and proud, still and silent, his attention focused, waiting for what has been promised.

Moses has been sitting like this, at the entrance of his tent, by day and by night, waiting for the first sign of the caravan that will bring his brother to him. Since beginning his vigil, Moses has neither eaten nor slept. His eyes are strained from looking, and his stomach aches with hunger. As the days pass, Moses fights a silent war within— alternatively hopeful and anxious, believing yet worried and impatient, too. When despair fights to win, he forces himself to remember the words of the Holy one, His promise to Moses, and His instructions, in their first days of intimacy on Horeb:

"Your brother will be your voice; send for him."

FIVE STONES AND A BURNT STICK

Even as he faithfully recalls these holy words, Moses senses that doubt and fear are beginning to take root in his heart. As he waits, Moses seems lost in a labyrinth of his own thoughts, his mind lurching frantically from the past to the future, neglectful of the present moment. His troubled mind wrestles with the past— viewing elements of it with extreme remorse and guilt—and wrestles with the future, too—fearful and apprehensive about what God's task for him may bring. "Aaron and I are brothers. We share the same blood. Yet our lives have been so very different. While I enjoyed a regal life of privilege and wealth, Aaron endured the hardship and penury of slavery. Born of the same mother, the fruit of our parents' love, our paths parted dramatically, and seemingly forever. But while destiny appeared to lead us along radically different paths, a greater power, the will of the Holy one, knew that we would one day be united, that one day we would once again walk together along His path for us."

To his neighbours, Moses appears subdued and serene, as he sits thinking at the entrance to his tent. But his outer composure belies the traumatic memories and emotions which rage within him. As he sits there, his mind's eye relives the terrible moment when he discovered the shocking truth of his real origin: he was not the child of an Egyptian princess, a member of the royal family; but, rather he—Moses—was the child of Hebrew slaves, saved from drowning in the Nile along with the other infant sons of the Hebrews, and this, only because Pharaoh's daughter had pitied him and taken him as her own. This discovery had turned Moses' entire world upside down: not a prince but a slave! This truth had utterly transformed him. He knew he must see these people as his own; but how and what would this mean? Dismay and bewilderment followed those dark days and yet ... Moses knew he must pursue the truth behind both his present, privileged life and his humble, Hebrew birth and rescue. And, with this thought, Moses felt rise from deep within him a promise, a strange, unexpected resolve: "I will face my past and find my family. These are my true people and I am theirs."

Every now and then, as he sits and waits, Moses talks aloud to himself and to the flies that circle around him. Gradually, without thinking, the details of this new story begin to tumble out of him in whispered confidences. "I was true to my promise," he murmurs. "And I acted quickly! I seized the first occasion and, accompanied by my bodyguard, made my excuses and crossed the city to the slave quarter to search for my true kindred. Upon sight of its wretched boundaries, I ordered my companion to come no further, instructing him to wait there for me, at the entrance. And then, despite his protestations, I entered this strange sector absolutely alone. I was convinced that to fulfil my purpose and find my true family, I must walk unattended through the strange and disturbing alleys of this place. Every glance told me that here outsiders were unwelcome and viewed with obvious—and understandable — suspicion. Every step deeper into the dark recesses of the Hebrew quarter, I sensed the mingled fear and hate which my royal Egyptian finery drew from those staring out at me from behind their cracked doors. And all my earlier confidence melted away. I felt increasingly ill at ease, awkward, and confused. Could I belong here? The anger and resentment these people felt towards me was palpable. I found myself struggling for breath in a stifling atmosphere which mixed fear and loathing in equal measure and hung like a miasma over this place. Nausea swept over me, churning my stomach, while chills wracked my body, betraying my unease. The oppressive presence of a living—yet deathly—fear rose up to meet me in every alley, seeped from every home and peered back at me from any soul whose eyes dared to meet my intruding gaze."

"This was the place about which I had heard so many stories. Revolts. Troubles. To all 'outsiders' it was a dangerous place, peopled by men without souls and without gods, who performed strange rituals that set them apart from all other men. A place of poverty and misery, inhabited by a despised race: the lowest of the low, the poorest of the poor. This was the place which Egyptians had learned to revile. And to fear. Walking through these streets, I both grieved and lamented the truth that it was here that I had been born."

Moses is gently roused from his painful reverie by Zipporah, who quietly comes to sit alongside him, wrapping her arms around his trembling, sweating shoulders to arrest their tremor. Zipporah seems to sense—even more than she knows—the brutal truth of the past Moses is now reliving and, by her presence, hopes to restore in her husband the loving, sensitive self which is also his. Moses grows still and then, comforted and sustained by his wife, begins again to relive this part of his life story, aloud, so that she can share it with him.

"I knew that my eyes were unprepared for the sight of so much suffering and deprivation, that my ears were unprepared for these wailing sounds of human distress, the howling of dogs and the strange shouts of children playing in those cramped alleys. Nor was my nose prepared for the fetid smell of the place—death, disease and the stench of open sewers hung thick in the air. My prince's hands were not prepared to touch these untouchable people, clad in filthy garments, tattered and torn beyond all decency. And, beyond my repulsion at so much physical misery lay the pain I felt as my own heart and soul struggled with the knowledge that the family who had given me life lived here and that at my birth had let me go, had given me away in unwilled abandonment. And this thought, the sad cruelty of it all, forced a sudden cry of unexpected desolation from my breast. I knew that I was prepared in neither mind nor body to meet these people—my family. And yet I also know that my unhappy heart longed to find them."

Meeting his true family and his brother Aaron swept away every comfortable notion of self which Moses had once enjoyed, and forced open his eyes to the oppression and abuse which lay behind Egypt's rule over his people. The harsh reality of what his slave family had to endure, on a daily basis, disturbed and unsettled him. Vivid images of the human misery suffered by the Hebrew slaves haunted his mind, waking and sleeping. And, though the overwhelming joy of meeting his true family was a healing balm for Moses' soul, explaining so much that he had never fully understood, the experience also overwhelmed him with a stifling guilt that his life of privileges—the life that he had "always" shared with those whom he had believed his princely family—had been funded by the blood, sweat and tears of his birth family and on the suffering of their people, his people.

Devastated by this truth, Moses had come gradually to realize that he could no longer live as he once had. He could no longer ignore the cries of humanity, could no longer escape the prompting of his overwrought conscience. And so, one morning as he had been walking about, sadly watching the Hebrews slaves at their labours, he caught sight of an Egyptian slave master beating one of his Hebrew brothers. Before he knew what he was doing,

FIVE STONES AND A BURNT STICK

Moses rushed towards the Egyptian and, in a moment of furtive, but unrestrained fury, killed the Egyptian and hid his body in the sand. But he had been seen, and from that moment on, Moses' life ceased to be his own.

The murder of the Egyptian transformed Moses into a hunted fugitive from a Pharaoh and from the very power which had once been the seal of his own privilege. Panicked, Moses fled, but had no place himself to hide. Terrified by his own passion and desperate for help from someone, Moses sought out the only person whom he knew he could trust: his new-found brother, Aaron. And Aaron had not failed him. He immediately welcomed his brother, and gave him a hiding place from which they could together devise an escape. With mounting apprehension the brothers waited for the moment when, under cover of darkness, they could slip out of the slave quarter, cross the city and pass the guards who watched its boundaries. The brothers now both feared for their lives—the one that he must now make his way back to the waiting family; the other that he must seek refuge in this wilderness, this trackless sea of sand where popular imagination believed the Leviathan lived.

In the last few anguished hours together, lingering at the boundary marking Pharaoh's sway and the vast emptiness of wilderness, Aaron and Moses forged deep bonds of brotherhood, friendship, and trust. And that day was the last that Moses had seen his Aaron face to face. Yet the words and images of their last meeting remained as vivid as life itself to the fugitive. And while he waited now, Moses rehearsed in his mind his own deep regret for what had happened. His last words, then, had been a kind of confession to Aaron, a confession Moses now intoned again in hushed whispers:

MY BROTHER

"I have brought deep shame on my family: I have stained my hands with blood. I have stolen another man's life. As a result of my action, I will never see you—or the rest of my family—again. Just when I thought that our paths might once more become one, we are now to be wrenched apart again."

His sense of shame and loss at their parting was so great that Moses felt, here in the wilderness around Horeb, as if he were standing once more before his brother, standing in Egypt. And then ... Aaron's response came to him, a response so vivid it now resounded in his ears: "Brother, I love you and Yahweh will show you the way."

Moses repeated Aaron's words aloud, and then suddenly realized that Zipporah had silently taken up her place beside him at their tent's entrance. And so, he turned to his wife and he shared the images so vivid in his mind:

"I remember suddenly dropping to my knees, and looking up into the kind eyes of my brother, Aaron. I then stretched out my arms to him, took his hands in mine, and guided them to the crown of my bowed head with a desperate cry, pleading: 'Bless me, Aaron! For with your blessing I will have all the strength I will need to face all that I must now live.'"

Zipporah could see that—in his mind's eye—Moses was again kneeling before his brother. She waited in silence for him to calm himself, knowing that her husband's trust in her, the intimacy that had long been theirs, now compelled him to tell her this story which would reveal to her the loving-kindness of the man for whom Moses now waited, the brother-in-law whom she had never met.

"Zipporah, Aaron did as I asked. He raised his eyes to heaven and solemnly prayed: 'May Yahweh bless and protect you every day of your life, and in His infinite mercy may He grant that my eyes will once more look into yours and that our family will again be reunited.' Zipporah, I had no idea who Yahweh was, but I believed my brother and trusted this blessing. And I trusted that his prayer of protection would enable me to face and endure the hardships ahead. His prayer gave me the courage to survive in this new life I was choosing, and the hope that one day I would be reunited with my brother, with my true people.

"'Goodbye, my beloved brother,' I whispered, embracing him, but in that last embrace I feared for him, too, for I could not know what my rash act might mean for him and the rest of our family. But Aaron reassured me: 'You will find a new life and we will be strengthened by the memory of having found each other and become true family.' And then we parted."

Moses fell silent once more, and Zipporah slipped away to leave her brooding husband to his vigil at the entrance of their tent. She could see him there, and knew that the Holy one could be trusted to work His ways in the mind and heart of her beloved husband.

As Moses lingered waiting for sight or sound of Aaron, a dark cloud eclipsed the sun, and fear obscured his heart once more. He recognized that creeping fear. It had been present within and around him ever since the day when the accusing finger had first been pointed at him: that day when his murderous blow felled the abusive Egyptian, the day when sudden compassion for his abused kinsman filled his heart, and this bewildering chaos of conflicting emotions had thrown his whole idea of himself into a near-permanent state of confusion and guilty fear. Each time this fear made its presence felt more keenly, it robbed him of himself and all peace. With downcast head and scarcely audible voice, Moses reflected: "The fear that I feel is a painful reminder that the Leviathan lives and has found a place deep within the darkest recesses of my soul and the souls of all mankind." But the wisdom of these words and his recognition of their truth did little to comfort him.

Moses no longer had a clear idea of how long he had been at his watch. Dusk and darkness had come once again, and now the dawn. He struggled against stiffness to upright himself after his long night's vigil, struggled against the weakness of his body and the accumulation of sleepless nights. He wondered how many nights might still lie ahead, and at the same moment vowed to remain faithful in his vigil, alert to the hope of Aaron's arrival. Wearily, Moses raised his eyes toward the horizon, sighed, and then … suddenly, the silence and stillness of the early hours, and the noisy turbulence of Moses' mind, body and spirit, were interrupted by the blowing of a ram's horn, the watchman's signal that a stranger was approaching! Straining forward, Moses discerned a solitary figure making his way toward the camp. Moses' agonized waiting was over. At last! His beloved brother Aaron!

The years of suffering and separation fell away in the joy of their reunion. The two brothers clung to one another, and in their embrace whispered thanks to the one who had heard their anguished prayers and restored them to each other. Days of celebration followed. Musicians and dancers were brought to welcome and entertain Aaron. Exotic delicacies and the best wine were set out to celebrate his coming. And Zipporah prepared exquisite pottages to set before her newfound brother, dishes lovingly prepared to celebrate his coming in accordance with her tradition. It was time now to eat and to drink, to celebrate, and to be grateful. A time to bless the day and to bless the Holy one. Theirs was a feast befitting the arrival of a king and everyone was invited—passing travellers, neighbours, and servants all attended. No one was excluded. All were called to celebrate.

For the brothers it was a time to rekindle their relationship and renew their knowledge of one another. A time to catch up with where they had left off, to relive old memories, to evoke past moments, and to tell and retell the individual and shared tales of their lives to any who would listen. And all those who heard them wondered at the joy and sorrow mingling so visibly on their faces.

Aaron had been with them many days before Moses finally found the courage to tell his brother why he had sent for him.

"Let us walk together, dear brother, dear friend," Moses suggested.

It was late afternoon and yet, once they had begun, the brothers walked for hours. They surveyed the oasis around which the encampment was built. They walked the labyrinths made by Zipporah's white stones in the sand. And, without sparing any detail, Moses told his brother all that had happened to him in this land around Mount Horeb, and of his encounter on its far side with the Holy one.

Aaron listened in silence, his attention and concentration unfaltering. Then, having heard Moses out, he asked with trepidation: "Brother Moses, are you asking me to be your voice?"

"Yes, Aaron. That is exactly what I ask of you."

"Am I correct in understanding that you want me to go with you to Pharaoh, the Egyptian king, as a messenger of the Holy one?"

"Yes, dearest brother. You have understood correctly. That is indeed the will of the Holy one."

"But, Moses! You are asking me not only to confront

the Pharaoh but also to confront the beast of fear within, the Leviathan itself. Tell me: what will you do if Pharaoh refuses to free our people? What will you do if his vile rage and fury are unleashed upon us and upon our people? What will you do when the Leviathan begins to carve your heart and burn your mind? Tell me, Moses. What will you do then? Run? By the time we realize our grave mistake, it will be too late. The Pharaoh will already have killed us and disposed of our bodies—or what's left of them—as food for dogs." Aaron's voice was full of fear.

"Dearest Aaron. I hear and understand what you are saying, but we do not need to fear the Pharaoh anymore: he is just a man. And as for the Leviathan … When I was on Mount Horeb with the Holy one, He revealed to me the wisdom which we will need to tame the Leviathan, to overcome its power." Moses' voice was earnest and yet completely calm.

"Brother, I find it hard to comprehend all that you are saying," Aaron replied honestly. He did not wish to hide that he was—all at the same time—confused, excited, and stunned by Moses' revelation and request.

"Aaron, I will tell you more as we journey towards Egypt," Moses replied confidently, a smile spreading across his face. And with tears of joy in his eyes, Moses embraced his brother. This first, most important, message from the Holy one now delivered, Moses and then Aaron, too, turned back towards the camp, their path illuminated by moonlight: Moses relieved and excited that the Holy one had given him the words to explain their mission, and Aaron—confused and yet excited by the conviction that it was the Holy one who had fashioned their reunion, and that it was He who had shown Moses that together, He wanted to use them both to redeem His people of Israel.

The Fourth Stone:
Disclosure

Everything seemed inert. Nothing seemed to move. It was as if the entire cosmic order had been put on hold. Time seemed to have ceased his reign and the entire world to stand still in awe and reverence, waiting in expectation for further glimpses of eternal truth and the disclosure of sacred wisdom. I, too, remained still and transfixed, standing in the same place, silent, unblinking, waiting together with the whole creation for the Holy one to reveal Himself anew from within the heart of the burning bush.

As I waited, I sensed an intense flow of energy surge through my entire being, from the crown of my head to the soles of my feet. I felt as if my spirit were soaring, as if my soul were glowing with the vibrancy of a sacred power. I began to tremble uncontrollably and felt my lips and tongue begin to move, forming the shapes and sounds of words not mine, but rather the syllables sung by angelic voices. Awestruck, I felt myself stagger at the sudden force of spiritual energy and began to sob, the tears welling up from deep within me, releasing all the sadness, all the sorrows, and all the fears and resentments that had burdened me for so long. I managed to stay on my feet for only a moment, and then fell to my knees before the deep and holy energy which was flooding my entire being. And then, yielding to its power, I fell prostrate on the dusty ground, silent and still, open to the torrent of energy within me. I remained conscious—my eyes, heart, and spirit open, fully present to all that was happening. And, as I trusted myself to this new reality, I gradually became aware that the intense energy pulsating through every part of my being carried the presence of the Sacred Spirit. Outside of time now, I sensed that my true self was being freed. Gently, layer after layer, the Sacred Spirit banished my deceiving spirits and plucked out the unhealthy roots of my self-deception. Gently, yet masterfully, the Sacred Spirit exposed my flawed nature, my wicked thoughts, my ruthless deeds and my feeble flesh. I was drenched with shame as I wrestled with the painful truth of my inadequacies, and yet I also knew that a miracle of cleansing and healing love was taking place within me, revealing the essential truth and essence of my own "I am". I then heard myself cry: "Holy one, have mercy on me. I am a man born of sin."

My prayer was met by more of His Presence. In silence the Holy one continued to delve deep within me, purging my entire being and, at the same time, embracing, strengthening, and reassuring me of His unwavering love:

"You are my beloved son. I created and have recreated you for a life of intimacy with me."

His words reached down into the very core of my being, their energy deepening my awareness of His Presence within me, until I sensed myself united with the Sacred one in love and intimacy. His Presence penetrated my skin and bones, my soul, my very essence. The cruel harshness of my misguided spirit and the hardness of my heart were gently swept away, as my soul was cleansed and I was filled with an ecstatic sense of peace, fearlessness and joy.

"We are one," I whispered, now totally convicted of this marvelous Truth.

I rested in His Presence, at peace. And then, something eerily mysterious seemed to emerge from deep within me and around me. I sensed a dark presence attempting to engulf, stifle, and overwhelm me. Nausea rose in my mouth and I gasped for breath. Blood—too much of it—jerked and jolted my panicked heart and, surging wildly through me, drummed mercilessly in my head. A dread I could recognize, but not name, overwhelmed me, and a cold sweat glistened, like the sea at dusk, over my shivering, shocked body.

At that very moment, the intense sacred energy faded and drained away from me and the experience of intimacy was replaced by a feeling of complete and utter desolation. I sensed the fearful darkness of the sacred absence, and with trepidation, I fully experienced what it is to exist without intimacy. Again—as many times before—I felt lonely, abandoned, afraid and totally annihilated. I desperately wanted to cast out the disturbing presence that seemed to overpower me. "But how can I overcome this nameless presence that lives and breathes within and around me?" I wondered. Fear and anguish filled my heart and, as I spoke, I became still more frightened.

"Holy one, please, I beg You. Save me from this evil presence, and release me from its destructive power over me!" My desperate plea appeared to hang unheeded in the air. Some time passed before the Holy one replied, simply, "Moses, I cannot do what you have asked."

The words crushed my spirit, obliterating all my hopes and unleashing an inconsolable grief in my soul.

"But Holy one," I cried angrily. "If you cannot master

THE FOURTH STONE: *DISCLOSURE*

this evil presence within me, then who can?"

"You, Moses. You can master the evil presence within you," the Holy one replied firmly.

"Me?" I cried in astonishment.

"Yes, Moses. You," the Holy one echoed in affirmation.

"But, Holy one. I do not understand. How is this possible?" My thoughts and questions were now more confused, frightened, and impatient than ever.

"Moses, what you have encountered is the Leviathan, the incarnation of fear. The Leviathan is the great mythical beast which all human beings must face, throughout their lives," the Holy one replied gently.

"The Leviathan?" I asked, intrigued.

"Yes. Before the creation of heaven and earth, when darkness and chaos ruled the universe, the Leviathan, the beast of fear, lived freely in the bitter waters of the sea and in the vast emptiness of a formless world. But when I created the world, light and order were born and I banished the Leviathan, locking him in the deepest recesses of the ocean floor. But then, your ancestor Adam succumbed to the lie that I could not be trusted, that my love had its limits, and that day the Leviathan regained his foothold on the earth. And from the moment he was released, Leviathan has scoured the earth, securing his awful place in the depths of the human heart and in the deepest folds of collective memory. And so, from one generation to the next, fear has been the blighted birthright of mankind; its fearsome birthmark has been the wounding contagion which all descendants of primal mankind have had to bear."

"But how long will mankind be prey to the Leviathan?" I cried anxiously.

"The Leviathan will prey on all the souls of mankind for as long as mankind walks this earth. only then, at the end of time, will the Leviathan finally be captured and locked up again forever. Until that day, the beast of fear—the curse resulting from mankind's first disobedience—will live on, tormenting and cursing every generation."

With despairing heart, my soul sank beyond hopelessness. But the Holy one, moved by compassion upon seeing my despairing state, continued: "My son, do not despair. Today I will entrust you with a secret."

"A secret?"

"Yes, my son. I will entrust you with the wisdom to overcome the Leviathan's power."

"But, Holy one, how can this be done?" I asked in amazement.

"Moses, you must listen attentively to all that I have to say. Listen with all your heart and mind. The first thing that you must understand and learn is that you cannot fight the beast. No-one can wrestle with the Leviathan and triumph. His power is beyond all human strength and all human control. You can only resist his power, until it lessens in intensity. Secondly, remember that you became aware of the Leviathan only when you were dwelling in intimacy with me. The knowledge and presence of the Leviathan is disclosed only to those dwelling in intimacy."

As the Holy one spoke these words of hope to me, I felt myself grow calmer. And as I waited on Him, my spirit began to comprehend that the power over the Leviathan was ultimately found within the love and mercy of the Holy one. And from my original despair, my heart rose to grow joyfully in hope for all of mankind and for the future.

"My son, listen to my words. When the beast, voracious as ever, arises from its hiding places to torment you, its assaults will be designed to wound you, to penetrate deep into your very self. Its breath of death will seek to poison

THE FOURTH STONE: *DISCLOSURE*

your mind and make you blind to the goodness and beauty all around you, to render you deaf to the poetry of the human soul and to the music of my created world. The Leviathan will seek to make you dumb in your attempts to speak out with your own true voice and numb to the sincere feelings of your own heart. But above all, the Leviathan will seek to prevent you from moving closer towards me, towards others, and towards true intimacy."

"Remember, Moses, the moment you sense its presence maligning your soul, be alert and stand your ground. You cannot escape from the Leviathan. If you want to subdue the beast, you have to face it. And as you face it, no matter what you feel, calmly take your stand safe in our place of intimacy. Hold your ground; root yourself in my promises, and then name the beast and all that it embodies. As long as the Leviathan remains nameless, it is untameable. But as soon as you name it and disclose its identity, you will bring it out from its dark, hidden place of terror and fear into the Light of all Truth. And, when Leviathan is in the light, you will discover that you have authority over it, and the power to tame it. Do not despair if the beast appears invincible. Do not surrender to its power. The longer you resist its poisonous grip of fear, the weaker the beast becomes, and the less power it has over you.

"Moses, you must trust in all that I have told you. But do not become complacent or be fooled by the beast. It is still the Leviathan and it is still the incarnation of fear. I tell you the Truth: the Leviathan will consistently and repeatedly attempt to poison your soul and the souls of all mankind. Do not be surprised by its attacks, but draw near to me and fear not."

The Holy one paused, letting me ponder His sacred wisdom before continuing. "My beloved son, be warned that prophet and priest, saint, mystic, and sibyl may all try to deceive you. You must not be deceived by any false promises of a life completely emancipated from the menace of the beast of fear. As long as you are alive, the Leviathan will try to make its claim upon you. Remember that intimacy is not a place where fear is absent, but a place where the beast of fear is disclosed, confronted, named, and eventually tamed and overcome."

At that moment, for the first time in my life, I had heard God's words on the Leviathan and come to a new understanding of its malicious power and the curse it attempted to inflict on all humanity. Overwhelmed with relief and with the profound truth with which I had been entrusted, I again broke down in tears. It was only then, on that day, that I recognized and appreciated the extent to which the sharp claws of the Leviathan were buried in my own soul, imprisoning me, and impeding my expression and experience of intimacy with all the beloved people in my life. As tears ran freely down my face, I gave praise and thanks to the Holy one.

"My beloved son, today you have learned the truth of life," said the Holy one. "Today, you have met the Leviathan face-to-face. Today you have learned that the great beast of fear is not simply around you, but that he also lives and exists within you. My son, today you have been enlightened with the wisdom that will enable you to overcome the gripping power of fear in your life. Live in the hope that one day the whole of humanity will be free from the beast of fear, and in the truth that, at the end of time, the Leviathan will be banished to the lake of fire where he will be tormented forever and ever. Moses, remember all that I have said. It will serve you richly in your life and on the journey that you must now travel."

THE FOURTH STONE: *DISCLOSURE*

"Dearest Holy one, your words will remain with me until the end of my days on this earth," I replied, with renewed strength of spirit and being.

V

Father and Son

The father and son did not wait for daylight; they knew that an early start would favour their intention of reaching the high point of Mount Horeb by midday. It was still dark when they began their gruelling ascent towards the summit of the mountain, leaving behind them a caravan of faithful men and camels, faithful servants all, snoring in unison and quite unaware that their master and his son Gerson had already arisen and begun their journey.

As father and son climbed, ascending slowly but steadily up the mountain, the land opened below them like a rare and precious flower before their delighted eyes. They made regular stops in order to stand and stare, immersing themselves in the glorious sounds and colours of early morning, and in a sunrise which clothed the vast firmament in a display of magnificent radiance. As day replaced night, God gently blew away the cobweb of mystery which had draped Mount Horeb to reveal all of the mountain's life and workings, displaying its dangerous and dramatic crags, revealing its awesome challenges, and stunning perspectives. As they climbed, father and son allowed themselves to be as one, immersed in all around them, aware—each in his own way—of the reverential awe rising up within him as they climbed ever higher.

They walked for hours, scaling sheer slopes, journeying along ancient paths which had been traversed by shepherds and runaways, outlaws, bandits, mystics and pilgrims since time immemorial. They walked without words, puffing and panting heavily, their hearts beating faster and faster as they toiled upward in the mounting temperatures of the day and concentrated hard in their effort to conquer the mountain's treacherous terrain and avoid its dangerous cliffs edges. They felt the soil beneath their feet disintegrate into hot clouds of dust around them, and heard loose stones cascade down the mountain below them towards the place where their journey had begun.

As they drew nearer the summit, both father and son felt their lungs searching frantically for the life-giving air which grew thin and strangely elusive there. Their bodies felt weak, their breathing laboured, and their movements cumbersome. Their strength and energy depleted, their legs, lungs, hearts, and spirits seemed ready to fail beneath the weight of heat and light and the physical demands the climb was making on them. Despite this, both father and son were resolute in their desire to journey upward and set their minds and faces toward their journey's end. And as they neared the summit, both man and boy quickened their pace, testing their bodies to the utmost, to face the final push to their destination. When they reached the crest of Horeb, the extent and beauty of the perspective it gave them left them speechless, overcome by wonder, and lost in praise. All their early pain and struggle was subsumed under a wave of heightened sensitivity and exhilaration.

But not even the rugged beauty of Horeb's heights could keep these climbers upright for long, and father and son soon tumbled to the dusty ground to rest their aching feet and limbs. After some time, the pounding of their hearts and heads slowed, their lungs relaxed and clear mountain air rushed strength into their lungs and bodies. Though remaining in companionable silence, Moses and Gerson eventually raised themselves from the ground to sit side by side on a boulder whose panoramic view invigorated both body and soul. The unique and precious moments which they shared there would inspire a joy which they would each carry to their grave and beyond. The majesty of the view surrounding them moved each one deeply, and they both sensed that here they were close to the Holy one, embraced by His infinite love, His beauty and His wisdom. Both father and son were profoundly grateful to have journeyed together and to have arrived at this sacred place, at the summit of Horeb. Horeb was deeply revered by many desert peoples and was known to many as the "Mount of God." Steeped in spiritual traditions, it was a place of myth, legend, and wonder which had fed the souls and imaginations of people for countless generations. And together at its summit, both Moses and Gerson felt that in its stillness they could discern the beating of God's own heart. Signs of earlier earthquakes signalled His Presence, and mountain showers carried strains of His lament. When storms blustered and blew, raking the mountain's face, a rainbow would give those who watched and waited the singular beauty of His smile of hope. This was a place where angels slumbered at midday, where the stars nested in the morning, and where night and day shared whispered words of love and intimacy. In this place holy men had traced their names, their hands outstretched to inscribe the dancing clouds. Mount Horeb offered men a glimpse of unearthly beauty, and to pilgrims a place of spiritual nourish-ment and companionable silence. From its heights the eye was rewarded by the sight of sleepy flocks, and among its scattered bushes a wilful wind prompted branches and flowers to dance to its singular music.

Moses had not been back to this place since the day he had encountered the Holy one in the blazing fire of the burning bush. But today, sitting with his son on a rock on the heights of Mount Horeb, he had returned to fulfil another promise: that one day he would guide his own dear son to the summit of Horeb. Today Moses had honoured his word to his beloved Gerson.

***

At midday the sun took centre stage, imposing its powerful and intense presence upon all living creatures. Moses and his son arose from the rock upon which they were sitting and sought refuge under the branched shade of a small tree, scarcely more than a shrubby bush. But in its shade, songbirds had found a haven and a gentle breeze stirred and refreshed the air.

"This is where we will break bread together," Moses told his son. And with this, he unwrapped their provisions: seasoned dried lamb, traditional herbs, bread without yeast, fresh figs, grapes, water, and a wineskin of wine that they had brought with them. Moses offered a prayer of thanks to the Holy one and they sat wordlessly together, eating contentedly in the shelter of this tree. Then, while Moses dozed, Gerson set off to explore their magnificent surroundings. He had never seen such beauty.

After a while, Gerson returned to the tree calling out excitedly to his sleeping father: "Father! Father! Wake up, wake up! I have found something!"

"What has happened?" Moses cried, startled from his sleep and alarmed by the shouts of his son.

"Father, I have found something! Come! Come with me! You have to see it!"

The excited boy was persistent, and eventually his sleepy, slightly disgruntled father got to his feet to be dragged towards his son's discovery. Gerson led Moses to a cave, whose entrance was obscured by overhanging branches but whose interior walls were covered by a large mural that reached back into the cave's darkest recesses.

"Look, Father! Look!" Gerson cried excitedly, shaking the sleeve of Moses' tunic and pointing animatedly towards the mural. But Moses remained calm, not sharing the excitement of his son.

"Yes, my son," Moses replied quietly. "I have seen it before, and it is indeed a sight to behold."

"But, Father! Do you think that this is the work of angels, or of the ancient giants who used to live here?" Gerson's questions tumbled out, drawn from a cache of folktales about Horeb which he had heard caravan visitors tell when he was a very young boy.

"No, my son. They did not do it. I did."

"You!" Gerson repeated with astonishment. "But how did you do it all, and when did you do it?"

"My dear son, sometimes when you are here, alone, in Horeb's isolated surroundings, far away from your home and family, the days and nights can seem almost unbearably long, and you grow lonely, weary, and bored. So, while the flocks slept, I would often come into this hidden cave, and on its walls paint my stories. At the beginning, I drew simply to distract my mind and pass the time. But gradually, I realized my paintings were drawing from me the story of my life. This mural is the work of many years of shepherding and of solitude here on Mount Horeb," Moses explained proudly.

"Father, it is beautiful! But is it finished?" Gerson asked, intrigued.

"No, my son. It will never be finished, not as long as I am alive."

No one other than Moses had seen this mural, and he wanted to ensure that his son fully understood the details and meaning of each picture. As the eyes of both father and son scanned each image, the mural's story—the story of Moses— began to evoke vivid memories from the past. Moses began to relive and remember the life of affluence and splendor that he had enjoyed while living as a child in the royal household, son to the daughter of Egypt's king. And then Moses recalled that terrible day when he discovered his true identity, forcing him to question who he was and where his true Hebrew parents and family might be.

As many times before, the cave's images rekindled powerful memories of his past, and re-ignited dormant feelings of anger, guilt and desperation. And, gazing again at one particular image, Moses felt impotent rage flare up as he focused on the tragic day when, in a moment of uncontrolled rage and revulsion provoked by the sight of an Egyptian beating a Hebrew slave, he had taken the life of the Egyptian and thus cast his lot forever with the Hebrew people. From that point on, Moses had become a fugitive from the very kingdom he had been trained to rule. He stood there silent, immobilized by the thought of all that had happened, but then...

"What is that?" Gerson asked, pointing to an image further along the cave's walls.

"That is the landscape of death and the wilderness," replied his father. Moses' memories of the wilderness were harsh ones. At one point he had even dared to dream that death would put an end to all his misery, and the terrible tragedy which engulfed his past and present. Yet even death eluded him, leaving him to wander seemingly endlessly in a hostile wilderness. But then …

"Is that you and Mother?" Gerson asked excitedly, pointing towards the image of a man and woman embracing.

"Yes," Moses replied, a gentle smile beginning to play upon his face. "That is the place where we first met."

"And is that me?" Gerson cried, pointing towards the image of a mother tenderly cradling her newborn infant.

"Yes, Gerson. That image is of you and your mother on the day that you were born. You were such a beautiful miracle in our lives," Moses explained with both pride and emotion.

As Moses answered his son's questions, the mural came alive to them both. All the feelings and emotions, memories and experiences of Moses' past were released from the prison of his defences, and once again he relived and experienced them as the present, but this time in the loving presence of his son. But the image which now most stirred him was of himself as a solitary shepherd surrounded by his flock. He remembered the pain and anxiety that accompanied the birthing process in his own life, as he struggled to embrace and accept the reality of his new desert existence. "I am no longer a prince in the courts of Egypt, but rather a solitary shepherd, a servant in the wilderness, with mountain boulders as my throne, a docile flock as my companions, the heavens as my advising councillors and this secret cave as my own place and palace."

As Moses followed the sequence of painted images, his attention was seized by the image of a radiant burning bush which was so real in its depiction that he marvelled at his own ability to express such a beautiful and awesome sight. The image of the blazing bush had been painted exactly in the middle of the mural, the centrepiece of his life story, its place and power proving that it was indeed the profound and cataclysmic event that had changed his life forever. Moses trembled as he remembered the moment when the Holy one first revealed Himself to him, and in so doing revealed to Moses the secret of his vocation.

"It was in the isolation of Mount Horeb," Moses whispered. "Far away from my home, family and civilization, far away from human counsel and the temples of religious teaching, that the Wisdom of Intimacy was revealed to me by the Holy one. It was in the isolation of Mount Horeb, dwelling here in intimacy with the Holy one, that I began to discover my true vocation, my own voice and my real vision."

Years had passed since that night when he had first discerned the unquenchable fire of that burning bush, but its light still flamed ever-bright within Moses' heart and within his spirit. And it was this light that since had illuminated his path, strengthening him and sustaining his resolve.

Moses and Gerson stood before the mural surveying its story together, and, as Moses studied it, he also looked into the face of his son and felt overwhelming love from him. Moses relished the opportunity to be with Gerson, alone in the stillness of this holy place, and for this moment dwelt gratefully, solemnly in his company, knowing that this might be the last time he would do so before embarking upon his journey to Egypt.

The boy feasted upon the vivid images crafted by his father, scrutinizing each detail of Moses' life as depicted in the mural's unfolding story. Moses himself was drawn back to the mural and realized that he, too, was astonished by this work of his own hands. And as he stood there, he revered the one who had inspired him to begin the mural, realizing the profound significance of a life story—not just for his family, but for the sacred mystery it revealed about all other human stories. Its truth showed Moses that his son's life was separate and different from his, and that Gerson would have his own dreams and aspirations, and that it was these which would fuel his life's journey. For the first time in all his years as a father, Moses recognized that he must let his precious son be free, that he must release him from all a father's hopes and expectations so that Gerson could do whatever he needed to be true to his own unique life's purpose.

Silently, tenderly Moses drew Gerson to him, gentling kissing the crown of his head. The boy looked up at his father and then, with his eyes fixed firmly on those of Moses, suddenly clasped his father to him, his hand tightly around his father's, overcome by sudden love, pride and respect for one who had come to see and draw such things.

Moses reflected, "In the eyes of my son I see a colourful tapestry of interweaving stories, of unknown men and women who began this particular story before he was even conceived. In his innocent eyes, which have not seen real evil or hardship, I glimpse the mingled threads of many others from which a new life will be fashioned. In his eyes I glimpse origins which go back to the beginning of all mankind. I see in his eyes the inheritance of love from the covenant that I made with his mother. And in his hands I touch a future which I can trust to the hands and voice of the Holy one who loves us both."

Moses and Gerson stood for hours before the mural. From the son tumbled question after question, reflecting his wonder and his curiosity. And to each response from his father the boy listened attentively, as if knowing each moment, each word between them was precious. Eventually Gerson had asked all his questions and the two again fell silent, the boy trusting his father and his answers. They each were simply content to be in one another's presence. And so they remained, a holy silence gradually permeating the very air of the cave.

After some time like this, Moses quietly withdrew, leaving his son alone in the cave while he sat in silence just beyond its mouth. Casting eyes about him, Moses took up a small stone and began to carve something onto it. Then, as the sun, too, withdrew its rays, Moses called out to Gerson: "My son. It is now time for us to return."

Gerson emerged from the cave and ran to embrace his father. "I will never forget what I have seen today, dear Father. The wisdom of what you have told me will remain engraved on my heart. Thank you! Thank you, dearest Father." Moses drew his son close and then stood, taking his hand in his so that together they could look together one final time at the serene perspective that lay before them. Then Moses knelt together with his son, and blessed the ground and gave thanks and praise to the Holy one.

As they made their way down the mountain, Moses' thoughts were with both his son and with the Holy one, praying that He would disclose His will to Gerson, too, and that one day Gerson would discover his true vocation, his voice, his dream, as Moses himself had discovered in his time on Mount Horeb.

The Fifth Stone:
Discovery

The flames from within the burning bush begin to intensify their display of changing colours and motion, patterns and form, while the wind pirouettes to share the dance with them. As the flames dance, I sense that the Holy one is not static and distant but rather active and engaging, present at all times and in all human endeavours. I am discovering a God whose abiding faithfulness is both unconditional and unreserved, a God who is moved to change His heart and remember His promises. The flames continue their hypnotically mesmerizing dance, and from deep with the bush the Holy one begins to speak again.

"Like this dancing fire, the stream of life has its own unpredictable ways that are unknown to the wise and learned, ways that cannot be found in temples or through oracles, and that are beyond the reach of seers and prophets. The secret of life is not written in the stars or on clay tablets or sacred stones. It is hidden in my memory, the Holy one. Only I have the knowledge and wisdom that can explain the secret of life, and only I choose those to whom this mystery, this secret, will be revealed. Moses, you have dwelt in my presence and I have begun to reveal

THE FIFTH STONE: *DISCOVERY*

to you the Wisdom of Intimacy, my dearest secret. Now you are one of the chosen few who live within this hidden world of intimacy." Overwhelmed by his words, I yet dared to ask Him: "But Blessed one, why me? Why me? I am unworthy of such grace and honour."

"I have chosen you because of a promise I made to your earliest ancestor," replied the Holy one. "At the beginning of creation I disclosed the divine secret to the primal man and woman on earth. But the secret was lost when, seduced by their own importance, they rejected my wisdom and followed ways of their own choosing. Their choice led them down the ways of sin, and away from intimacy with me. This choice brought chaos and death upon the earth where they have reigned in the lives of each succeeding generation. Since that day, humanity has spent much of its time in despair and suffering, bewildered and lost in its own desperate devices.

"My heart is broken. I grieve deeply when I see my beautiful creation in a state of such ugliness and disarray. Moved by humanity's suffering, I one day promised my faithful servant Abraham that I would reveal to his descendants the lost secret, and that they would become the entrusted custodians of that secret until the time came for it to be revealed to the whole of humanity. Today, Moses, I have begun to reveal that lost secret to you, and that secret is the path of intimacy. As you continue on this sacred path, you will realize that intimacy is a journey of discovery."

"Discovery?" I echoed nervously.

"Yes, Moses, discovery. In the experience of intimacy you will discover your own true 'vocation,' 'vision,' and 'voice.' My dear son, intimacy is a lifelong walk of continuous discovery. As you dwell in intimacy, you will learn to trust that life has meaning, and you will be empowered in all that you do with me.

Without necessarily knowing everything, you will begin to see a pattern of continuity emerging. As you grow in intimacy with me, you will also grow in intimacy with others and with your own authentic, innermost being. When you begin to experience that intimacy, you will be able to hear the voice of life calling out to you, beckoning you to follow your own life's truth path. Rather than being persuaded to follow the vocations of others, you will feel compelled to pursue your own true vocation. This vocation is hidden beyond the interests of money, power and lust, and is rooted in the depths of your free soul."

"Remember, Moses, your soul is at its freest and most true when it dwells in intimacy with me. Think of all the times in the past where different voices have tried to contradict and confuse you, telling you where to go and what to do. But as you journey on the path of intimacy, you will grow in awareness and conviction of your own true vocation, purpose and understanding in life.

"When you find your true vocation, you will also discover your own voice; then you will be able to speak the truth. Your own voice is the sound of your soul, the reflection of your own divine image, and the fruit of the divine Spirit that resides deep within your true inner being. Your own voice is not a sound that you make with your vocal chords, but the awareness of your own presence as you make a stand for your own truth and your own convictions. Remember that your own voice is the assertion of your own true passions, the honest revelation and expression of your own soul, the giving of yourself with selfless devotion, and the echoing of my own voice. When you discover and use your own voice, then you will know its power to bless and curse, to accuse and forgive, to

THE FIFTH STONE: *DISCOVERY*

comfort and reprove, to nourish and condemn, and to rebuke and heal.

"As you discover your real vocation and your own voice, you will discover your true vision. This true vision is born and nourished in intimacy, and will become the passion that drives you towards your destiny. This true vision will sustain you through all of life's adversities and obstacles, and will enable you to grow in faith and to live in hope whatever your situation or circumstance. As you follow the path of intimacy, your vision will grow and mature and will carry you to the places where you will experience, learn and grow.

"My beloved son, without vision, you will perish; without your own voice, you will be a cacophony of other voices; and without your own vocation, you will be directionless."

"Holy one," I respond humbly. "The seeds of your wisdom have found fertile soil in my heart. Now I am at last beginning to grasp that life is a mystery that is not easily explained or understood, and that life is bound up with ambiguity and lack of clarity because it withholds more than it reveals. In intimacy, I have learned to honour mystery. Now I have begun to realize the importance of discovering my vision, vocation and voice, and to appreciate your miraculous power to move us beyond our human limitations or social circumstance towards the realm of the impossible, the supernatural and the spiritual."

"Indeed, my beloved son," the Holy one continued. "As you dwell in the wisdom of intimacy and of your senses, instincts, intuition, soul, heart, mind, body and spirit, you will become increasingly aware of the meaning of the signs and unpredictable movements which are inherent in the stream of life. Then, Moses, you will understand that life is not an accident of chance, or a compilation of unconnected events directed by nameless fate. You will see that life is a tapestry of connected events with innate purpose and direction. It is only as you make the journey of life in intimacy that you will see and understand the interconnections which will give sense and meaning to the events in your life, and a sense of validity and continuity to your story. The journey of intimacy and all that it evokes, exposes, develops, expresses and creates will make your daily experiences significant, purposeful, and transcendent.

"Since leaving Egypt, you have desperately sought for an experience of connectedness, of purposefulness, meaning and validity in your life. Now you will begin to discover these more fully and, as a result, find yourself increasingly at peace, content, self-expressing and self-fulfilled. Remember, Moses, that the purpose and integrity you seek is made up of the indivisible threads that bind life together and make it true and meaningful. It is only in intimacy that you will truly discover, experience, and understand these sacred threads."

The words of the Holy one filled my entire being. I knew that in sharing with me the mystery of intimacy, the Holy one had spoken words which opened my world out to cosmic dimensions, giving my existence clear direction and purpose and giving me the conviction that all life can be lived as an organic, evolving story. For the first time in my life I could see the signs of continuity amidst the labyrinth of contradictions, and I could see, too, the connections among what, in the past, I would have mistakenly considered useless, irrelevant, disconnected fragments of brokenness. I could not explain the reason for the many things that had brought pain, devastation, and grief in my life, but the mists clouding my understanding were fast

THE FIFTH STONE: *DISCOVERY*

fading as I began to discern the broad outlines of God's master plan.

I know that I have made many mistakes and have dreamt up deluded, self-deceiving visions which have obscured my life's path. But now I am persuaded that the pure stream of life has always found me when I thought myself most lost, and that it has carried me in its flow towards this intended encounter with the Holy one. Now, having heard the words of the Holy one, I am blessed by the holy conviction that, whatever the future holds, I am indeed truly following my life's journey, and that in this I am ultimately following His will for me and for His people. I am now ready to journey to Egypt and to command the most powerful king on earth: Let my people go.

"Holy one," I responded, trusting, loving Him completely. "I now understand all that you have told me. Today I have learned that true discovery, true being, exist only in the realm of intimacy with you."

VI

The Last Night

Zipporah

"Tonight is our last night," she whispered into the air, struggling apprehensively against the desperate thought of his absence soon to come and yet moved, as always, by the intense joy of his presence with her now. She longed for this night to last forever and yet felt it rushing heedlessly on, as if the uncertain future were determined to drive them apart. She calmed herself—for his sake as much as hers—and whispered again, "Tonight is our last night."

Incense smouldered in its burner, perfuming the air with its exotic aroma, but her disquiet refused to dissolve into the deepening shadows of approaching darkness. As they lay beside one another, the oil lamps flickered out, one by one, as if they, too, sighed at the coming of night's sway. And at that moment the blurred shadow of two lovers embraced one another and, in a sleepy mutual consent, surrendered to the call of night. Safe in the warmth of her husband's arms, Zipporah murmured once more, "Tonight is our last night," and then, "tomorrow you will be gone."

Inwardly, she tormented herself with thoughts of her beloved taking leave of her, greeting the dawn as he

THE LAST NIGHT

embarked upon his long, gruelling journey to the land where he had been born to be reunited with his family there, with his own people. She knew that he would be revisiting memories that he had tried to leave behind, and a past that he could not forget. Silently she agonized over thoughts of how long he would be away, and when—if ever—she would see him again. Silently, too, she vowed her eternal love and loyalty to him, "Tomorrow you will be gone ... perhaps forever. I will pray for you and I will wait for you. Our wedding ring will remind me that we are bound by our love, and that we truly belong only to each other."

In the inviting darkness, she began to run her fingers through his greying hair, caressing his face, tracing the lines drawn by the years, marks left by the changing seasons of time and fortune. She knew that the years had diminished his robustness, but she also knew that her husband retained the courage, spirit, and fiery determination of his youth. And if his body had aged, it had done so with dignity and grace, and he had grown in wisdom. Her dear Moses was handsome still, his eyes and spirit retaining all the charm, all the virility of his young man's days.

"His are the eyes of a vibrant, travelled, and journeying wise man," she thought. "They are windows onto the soul of a man who is honest, truthful, seeking. Sometimes I look at him and see reflected in his eyes the fresh, insatiable curiosity and vivacity of the young man I first knew. But at other times I see eyes that are cloaked with the sadness of a wounded man, who has seen too much excess, too much suffering and injustice in life. But beyond the sadness, I often see in the laughing eyes of my beloved soul survivor the joyful blessedness of one gifted with extraordinary creativity, a mystery that makes my soul celebrate, and my heart dance. This precious gift was present the moment I first looked into his eyes, and I can see it still these forty years since. I will never forget the intensity of our meeting and the blazing fire in his eyes."

The day of their meeting! Etched on her memory, rehearsed in detail when time gave her idle moments, cherished in long days and nights when shepherding took him away from her, that day lived on as it were today. She had revisited it, reliving the passion that sprang up in her—sprang up in them both—and told the story of their meeting and marriage so many times before. And it grew more cherished in each telling.

"I had gone to the well with my sisters, to draw water for my father's flock, when some wicked shepherds tried to take advantage of us. The men terrified us, and as we tried desperately to defend ourselves against them, another man—a tall, handsome, imposing figure—appeared as if from nowhere to help us. He charged towards the shepherds, his arms flailing and his voice growling out at them to leave us alone. The shepherds ran in terror. My sisters also ran away, back to the safety of my father's camp, back to tell our father what had happened. But I remained. All was quiet and stillness and this man—a stranger, our protector—and I were left standing together alone. I shyly thanked him for his help and chanced to see that he was studying my face, smiling warmly but wordlessly.

"Then, he noticed that my hand was bleeding from a scratch suffered in my struggle with the shepherds, and so he gently bathed it with clean water from the well, and then dried and bandaged it with a piece of soft cloth. As his warm, strong hand encompassed mine, I looked into his eyes and felt the fire of love and desire begin to awaken within the deepest part of my body, heart, and spirit. I felt as if a mysterious force were drawing me nearer, closer to him. I did not resist.

"My father understood this and, at his request, the stranger was welcomed into our camp and life, and I was offered to him in marriage. I surrendered to the wisdom of life and let myself be carried in its stream towards a blessed union with the man who had found and rescued me. While I had known nothing of the man who stood before me by that well, my heart had immediately realized that he was my life's love. In that moment, I was truly blessed by the Holy one. The fire of love and life was kindled at the moment of our meeting and has burned vibrantly ever since. We have journeyed much together, but still the fire lives on, strong and true."

"Tonight is our last night," she whispered again to her beloved. But this time he gently cupped her face in his hands and silenced her lips with a gentle, lingering kiss. They gazed deeply into each other's eyes, immersed in the eternity of their limitless love and union, defying all tomorrows in order to exist fully in the blissful, eternal present they now shared. Words became redundant as they began to converse with their hands and bodies. His warm, strong hands, calloused from hard labour, gently caressed her soft skin, and his long, creative fingers playfully traced imaginary figures on the length and breadth of her body. In that instant she fleetingly remembered her beloved telling her: "When I am with the flock on Mount Horeb, I sometimes grow bored and lonely. To help me pass the long nights, I often go to a cave and draw the story of my life in pictures on its walls. I have created a great mural and one day I will take you there and show it to you." In one part of her consciousness, she realized that that day might never come, and she might never again see her beloved. Suddenly, she felt an overwhelming desire to see his art that very night and at that very moment. In the infinite yet finite gift of this, their last night together, she longed to know all his love, all his being, and all his creativity.

It is an ancient tradition among the women of the desert to decorate themselves with special body paints, paints which they apply to embellish their bodies for special occasions, like on the night of their wedding. This ritual of beautifying the body by drawing patterns had always been done between women, but this night Zipporah felt inspired to break the tradition, to alter the old ritual.

"Moses," she blurted out impulsively. "Please do a drawing on my body, as I am now, lying naked with you." Moses laughed, thinking that the wine they had shared had confused his wife, disordering her thoughts.

"Tonight is our last night. Please draw a picture from your life's story on me!" she pleaded.

Moses looked at Zipporah, puzzled and yet pleased by her request. "Are you really certain that you want me to do this?" he asked, genuinely surprised, and fully aware of the tradition they would be breaking.

"Oh yes!" she replied earnestly.

Moses looked lovingly at Zipporah and—without saying a word, and yet without hesitation either—he acceded to her entreaties. "Tonight is our last night." He smiled sadly and tenderly at her. "Let us make the very most of it."

Moses

"Tonight is our last night," he gasped, his voice choked

with emotion, his heart gripped with the desperate fear that he might never again see his beloved Zipporah. "Tonight is our last night." His sad, pain-laden words melted into the heavy scent of her perfume and the aroma of burning incense. The oil lamps guttered and gave up their last breath of light as darkness became their host, inviting the lovers to embrace the shadows of the night. He wrapped strong arms around her, drawing their bodies together in perfect unity. They lay as one, devastated and terrified by the knowledge that they might never again spend another night together. Moses wanted to reassure her, to tell her that all would be well; but he knew that the future was uncertain—uncertain save the certainty of danger. He had no vision of how long he would be away, nor when, or if, he would ever again see his beloved wife. He lay stretched out beside her, struggling silently, alone with his desperate thoughts.

"Tomorrow, as the new day awakens, I will embark on the long journey back to Egypt, to my homeland. For days and nights I will travel through inhospitable desert and wilderness until I reach the city where I was born and grew to manhood. Aaron will travel with me and share all the journey's trials, but still ... I am troubled, frightened. I feel deeply uneasy and, yes, terrified. The thought of what lies ahead has awakened the darkest fears within me. The mere idea of confronting Egypt's Pharaoh almost destroys me. Tomorrow I will be gone. And my only certainty is the intimacy I share with Zipporah and with the Holy one who brought us together. I will take her lifelong love and prayers with me each step of this new journey, and carry her love, her ways and the image of her dear face in my heart wherever the Holy one leads me. These rings we wear will be the sign of the covenant between us, and of the vows we have made to love one another for as long as we both shall live."

"Tonight is our last night," he whispered again, but this time his words were arrested by the sight of his beloved, her face and form mesmerizing him. He mapped her in the darkness of the tent, rejoicing that the years had served only to enhance for him the physical and spiritual landscape of her being. In all their years together she had given him her constancy, her companionship, her wisdom, and all the joys of married love and affection. While she was no longer the young girl he had first encountered by the well, Zipporah had blossomed in their life together, radiating a new, inner beauty which made her yet more attractive in his eyes. Her figure was now sculpted by time; her curves enhanced as her body had grown to accommodate the fruit of their love. He saw the changes that time had visited upon her as the seasons and years had passed; he saw the silver that now streaked her dark hair and the lines her laughter had drawn about her eyes. But for Moses her body retained all the grace and distinction that it had ever borne. With time Zipporah had grown intensely beautiful and wise, and yet she was to him as open-hearted and guileless as the day he had first cast his eyes upon her.

"I remember so clearly the day I first saw her standing by that well. She and her six sisters had come to draw water for their flock, but some wretched shepherds had frightened the girls and were chasing them. I heard their desperate cries and immediately ran to their rescue. The shepherds fled in cowardly haste, and so did Zipporah's sisters. They ran back to tell their father that a 'strange Egyptian' had rescued them from wicked men. But Zipporah remained. Suddenly this beautiful girl and I found ourselves alone together. I felt self-conscious and awkward at this sudden intimacy, but then noticed that her hand was badly scratched and bleeding. Without a word, I gently bathed it with fresh water from the well. Slowly and carefully I dried her beautiful hand with my garment and felt her delicate fingers, one by one, through the cloth. Her head was bent as I bandaged her hand, but when I had finished she looked up at me and I permitted myself to look into her eyes. At that moment, I felt a burning desire and impulse to be with her forever. I did not then even know her name. She was a stranger to me, but somehow I felt as if I had always known her and as if we would always belong together. A powerful and mysterious force drew me towards her. The fire of love that was kindled that day continues to blaze, its light illumining my days and nights, warming my heart, brightening the way."

Tonight the same hand he had taken and bandaged so many years before now guided him to the task of painting his story on her body. She recalled the stories he had told her about the large mural he drew in the caves on Mount Horeb. She remembered, too, his promise to one day take her there. But he, in the darkness of this their last evening together, was filled with a wondering fear that perhaps that day might not now ever come. Lost in the thought of his disorientation without her, he was surprised when, gently gesturing, she yielded herself to his artistry. All his hesitancy disappeared the moment he realized that this drawing was what she truly desired. When she repeated her request, indeed, pleaded with him, he could no longer refuse her. "Tonight is our last night," he said, his heart overflowing with love for her. "Let us together make the most of it."

FIVE STONES AND A BURNT STICK

Zipporah & Moses

"Tonight is our last night," they whispered in unison, defying the morrow, rejoicing in this night they would now live together. The morrow's heartache, then as now, would be enveloped in the truth of this shared reality, the life and love and creativity, the mystery of their intimacy which had been and always would be the Holy one's greatest gift to them as man and wife.

Moses took an oil lamp, relit it and placed it on a tabouret nearby. Then, taking a small hessian bag from his shepherd's pack, he drew out a burnt stick, whose end would serve as pen, and a small packet of black charcoal powder to mix with oil to make his ink. He smiled at Zipporah, prepared his drawing instruments and then began his sketching, her body his canvas. With fluid yet firm lines he drew a hill, a well, trees, the sun, the moon, a shooting star, a flock of sheep, a single shepherd, and a woman with a boy, all of these upon the landscape of her body that now became his artist's surface. Moses became totally absorbed in his creation, working skilfully, confidently. And as she watched him Zipporah realized that the Holy one had blessed her husband with a great creative gift. Her eyes saw him with a tenderness seasoned by the lifetime of companionship they had already shared. From time to time she reached out and gently stroked his hair, smoothing the wayward locks from his eyes, hoping to aid his concentration and remind him of her utter devotion to him and her love.

"My beloved, please stay still and do not move. I will be finished soon, I promise."

He spoke as husband, but as artist, too, concerned that her movements might spoil his drawings.

THE LAST NIGHT

"I cannot stay still. Your drawings are tickling me!"

They both exploded with laughter. The bubbling brook of their shared laughter celebrated their complete intimacy and love for one another. It also acted as a release for the vast sea of desperate feelings and emotions which they had tried to suffer in their separate silences. Their laughter was healing music, a balm to their ears, hearts and spirits, which broke down all fear's terrible barriers, and swept them towards the joy of union and filled their tent with the enveloping aroma of incense and their love.

"Will you keep the drawings until I see you again?" he whispered.

"Perhaps ... perhaps," she replied, a love-drenched smile spreading across her face.

Soon Moses finished his drawing. He replaced the burnt stick in the hessian bag and waited for the ink—still wet upon her body—to dry.

"Is that me?" she asked, pointing at the figure of the woman, drawn sitting under a tree, beneath the sun and stars he had painted just below her navel.

"Yes," Moses replied lovingly.

"But I am not that curvaceous!" she protested, laughing and teasing him.

"Well, I told you to be still!" replied her husband, gathering her up in his arms and examining his artwork closely on the beautiful skin of his beloved.

His drawings had become a celebration of life and creativity, of love and desire, and of their profound trust and intimacy. Together in the dark and silent night, their bodies and spirits danced to the images and music of their love for one another. That night they shared total, abandoned intimacy. The laughter, joy and passion which they shared so intensely that night were like none other in all their years of marriage. Finally, satiated and exhausted, they rested quietly in one another's arms, the tent pregnant with their joy and love for one another. They breathed each other's breath and very essence, and gazed up through an opening in their tent to feast together on the beauty of the night sky, its stars shining with possibility. Eventually, they could fight sleep no longer and fell into a deep slumber, wrapped in each other's arms.

And so they remained until their waking. Just before dawn they stirred and smiled at one another, sharing these last tender moments together before rising to face together the new day and all it would bring.

"My beloved Moses, life has graced us with many beautiful years together," Zipporah breathed, smiling and tearful. "We have known each other, completely and honestly, for who we truly are. We have seen the passing seasons of our souls and endured the sorrows of difficult days. We have witnessed the flaws in our characters and know the weaknesses of our flesh. We have seen what no one else has seen of us, and know the secrets of one another's souls. In accordance with our sacred covenant, we have kept true and faithful to one another. But, since your return from Mount Horeb, we have found a new-shared intimacy with one another; we have found ourselves in a new way of being with one another and have created a sacred place, a fertile, nurturing loving paradise in which to grow and be. We have, in truth, become the blessed home of one another's soul!" With these words, Zipporah kissed Moses and drew him tightly to her.

"My beautiful Zipporah," Moses responded. "The mystery of life and the sacred fire placed in us by the Holy one have brought and kept us together. The fire that burnt brightly at the beginning of our encounter with one another

THE LAST NIGHT

has remained burning brightly within us ever since. I was ignorant of its presence. But now I recognize and know it, for in the hills of Horeb I learned about the sacred fire and about the path of true intimacy. Let us keep the flame of love, life and desire burning brightly within us as we walk together on the path of intimacy.

"Let us draw the boundaries of love, let us rejoice in our differences, and dwell in each other's presence. Let us acknowledge and disclose the power of the Leviathan, of the fear within us, and together discover—each one—our own unique voice, our true vocation and our real vision. Let us renew our covenant to one another now, this very moment. And let us commit today to the path and wisdom of intimacy that have been revealed to us by the Holy one." Moses' words were fervent, and they were inspired.

Zipporah's response was immediate: "I belong to you and you belong to me."

"My beloved, we belong to each other!" Moses replied solemnly.

"Together we belong to the Holy one!" they affirmed simultaneously, together in union of love, being, and spirit.

***

Long before dawn, the servants had arisen to complete the preparations for the long journey which lay before their dear master. They had worked in silence to preserve the peace of his last moments with Zipporah. But at last, everything was ready for the travellers. The camels were laden with all the water and provisions that they would need for the long journey ahead, and all in the camp had begun to assemble to bid Moses and Aaron farewell. When the time came for them to depart, the watchman blew his ram's horn to signal that all was in readiness. All of the servants gathered. They stood together, a sheltering wall of faithful friends, alongside Zipporah and the Master's beloved son, Gerson. One by one, Moses greeted and blessed each of them by name and took their proffered hands in his. When Moses came to Gerson, he lifted his son in his arms and held him tightly to his chest, whispering words of love and wisdom in his ear. Setting him down, Moses anointed Gerson's head with aromatic oil and prayed blessings over him. And then, finally, having bid farewell to everyone else in the camp, Moses embraced Zipporah, his most cherished, beloved Zipporah. They clung to one another, kissing deeply and with a love so intense that all who beheld could not hide the tears in their eyes, nor the pain they felt at their separation.

Drawing on his deepest reserves of courage and self-control, Moses finally pulled away, better to look deep into the eyes of his beautiful wife and to give her something he drew from his cloak.

"My beloved Zipporah, if something prevents me from returning to you, you must give this hessian bag to our daughter to keep it safely."

"Daughter? But we have no daughter," Zipporah replied, confused.

"We will," Moses replied with conviction. "Last night I dreamt that the Holy one will bless us with a daughter." Then, gently placing his hands on his wife's abdomen, Moses prayed, "May the Holy one bless our daughter as she grows in her mother's womb."

Zipporah flung her arms around her husband and wept tears of joy and sorrow.

"It is time for us to go," Aaron urged his brother, mounting on his own camel.

THE LAST NIGHT

Moses and Zipporah gazed once more into one another's eyes.

"I know that I will see you again," she said, smiling with utter conviction. "For I also had a dream last night, a vision from the Holy one, in which with my own eyes I saw you leading your people through the wilderness towards the Promised Land."

The Burnt Stick
The Sacred Fire

As the fire within the burning bush rose and fell to the music of the wind, the flames began at last to die back. Unmoving, Moses watched a column of grey smoke, coloured with tones of light and sparks of fire, begin its unhurried ascent toward heaven.

"It is the end of the fire," he told himself as he watched the once blazing bush turn to smouldering grey ash and blackened wood.

"Moses, the sacred fire never ceases," the Holy one replied to my thoughts, disrupting them and teaching me that He is always the intimate companion of my mind and heart. "You must know that the sacred fire burns within you." "Within me?" I repeated, uncomprehending.

"Yes, Moses. Within you," the Holy one declared. I listened to the sound of his voice, and found myself shaking like an autumn leaf trembling in the wind.

"Moses, the Sacred Fire has always been within you, from the moment that you were born into the world."

"But, Holy One, how is it possible I was never aware of its presence within me?" I asked, confused.

"Indeed, you were not aware," the Holy one replied. "Moses, you grew up in a patriarchal world that has quenched the presence of the Sacred Fire and denied its purpose, which is to guide you toward the path of intimacy. That is why so many humans live unaware of the path of intimacy—oblivious to the Sacred Fire within them."

"Holy one, how can we awaken to the Sacred Fire within us and be led to the wisdom of intimacy?" I asked gravely.

"Do not fear, Moses. All humans have their opportunity, a brief instant of awakening, a moment of grace when the force of the Sacred Fire offers them the possibility to be guided towards the intimacy that I intended from the beginning of creation. It will enable them to overcome the dogmas of patriarchy. Sadly, not all humans seize their opportunity and instead make other choices, ignoring the spontaneous guiding force of the Sacred Fire."

"But why do people choose otherwise?" I asked, heavy with sadness.

"Moses, you were not the only shepherd on Mount Horeb tonight. There were many others scattered around, and all of them saw the fire. Only you, only you, Moses, let the force of the Sacred Fire within guide you to the burning bush. Why you and not the others?

"A long, long time ago, you rescued seven girls from cruel shepherds at a well in Midian. Six of the girls ran home. Only one remained. Why did Zipporah stay and not one of the others? Why? Zipporah recognized the movement, the moment of grace. She responded to the sacred fire within and joined the sacred fire in you.

"Equally, you were not the only one around the well that day when the seven daughters of Jethro cried out for help. There were other men nearby, but only you went to their rescue. Why you and not the others? You and

Zipporah let the force of the Sacred Fire guide you towards each other, towards intimacy. You trusted in the force within you without knowing that it was the sacred fire leading you towards one another, towards intimacy. Tonight you again seized your moment. You let the Sacred Fire within guide you, and as a result you have discovered me from within the burning bush, and in your response you have perceived the secret of intimacy now revealed to you. People have their opportunities, their moment of grace to be lead by the Sacred Fire, and each one makes their choice," the Holy one replied solemnly and then fell silent, allowing me to digest his sacred words, before continuing to speak to me from the dying fire of the burning bush.

"Moses, as you follow the path of intimacy you will grow increasingly in awareness of the Sacred Fire within you. But you will never fully know its secret, its mysterious ways, its blessings and properties and its many manifestations and virtues. The Sacred Fire reveals itself according to its own timing and choosing. All these are an unveiled mystery. The sacred purpose of the fire is to lead people to intimacy with one another and with me. That is all you need to know. When the Sacred Fire leads you towards the other, towards intimacy, it will also lead you to make covenants where intimacy can be fostered and protected, covenants which will allow intimacy to grow and flourish.

"My beloved son, when you chose to respond to my call from within the heart of the burning bush, you first recognized me. You were drawn to me, to intimacy, by the sacred fire within you."

"Holy one, I long to make a covenant with you. You will be my God, and I will listen to you and walk on the path of intimacy every day of my life, from today until the day that I die," I cried out with all of my being.

"Moses, you belong to me and I will belong to you and we will dwell in the mystery of intimacy from now and through all eternity," the Holy one responded. And this time the power of his Word resonated throughout my entire being.

I drew closer to the fire's embers, realizing that the burning bush was now present to my eyes only in the hot grey ash and a lone burning stick. Even so, I longed to remain near its warm presence until the very end. I knelt on the ground and gathered up some of the black ash which the fire had left, and scooped it into a cloth pouch around my waist. I knew already that I would make ink with this black dust, and that I would use the burnt stick, which had earlier helped me to encircle my sacred space, as an instrument for drawing. With both the black dust and burnt stick in my hessian bag, I sensed that the ending of this first encounter with the Holy one marked the very beginning of a lifetime's encounter with Him and others in true intimacy.

Epilogue

Miriam studied the now-still face of her beloved father. Though silent to this earth in death, his voice with its last, wise words of intimacy continued to whisper their truth and the reality of their love audibly in her heart and head. "He is not here," she thought. "He journeys now, united with the Sacred Wind. And he has left me this small hessian bag as a sign of his presence, as symbols of the sacred truths he has entrusted to me."

Miriam glanced down at the bag in her lap, and then gently reached over to her father and folded his gnarled old hands in the posture of prayer she had seen him adopt so many times before. His hands, which had been raised to lead his people for so many years, now lay at rest, clasped together in hard-won but joyful trust in the Sacred one whom he worshipped. His eyes were already closed, as if to keep the visions in. But his love was there and so was his hessian bag—this precious spiritual daughter's inheritance reserved for her.

Miriam sat beside her father, gazing for some time at his dear face, her hand on the object in her lap. And then, purposefully, she opened the bag. Inside it she found five stones and a burnt stick, along with a message from her father, written in black ink on a pure white lambskin. The message read:

THE BURNT STICK *THE SACRED FIRE*

"My beloved Miriam,

The Holy one has shown me that one day my people's kings and priests will overcome the prophets. These rulers—without knowing the Holy one, without ever glimpsing the joy of relationship—will use religion to dominate and control my people. Priests and kings will pervert the message and spirit of the Holy one, constructing corrupt temples and teaching a religion of strict dogma and law, which will delude my people and present the Holy one as a god whom they should serve in fear and placate in blind obedience.

"I have been shown that men of corrupt hearts and minds, who have never experienced the Sacred Fire within, will use their authority to enforce a patriarchal hierarchy where intimacy will have no place. And in that society the Holy one will no longer dwell in the hearts and temple of His people. He will become as if a Stranger amongst them. But, my beloved Miriam, the Holy one in His goodness has granted me a further vision. One day a woman will bear in her womb a prophet of God—one called 'the Son of Man'—who will disclose to all mankind the lost way of holy intimacy. The woman will feed him with the sacred dream. Her heart will open to Him the secret wisdom of waiting in trust for the Sacred one's love and Truth. She will support her Son as He learns to walk with God, for it is He who will lead all of mankind along the lost way of love. His coming will herald the beginning of a new era, when all men and women will share this sacred wisdom again.

"Until that day arrives, my dear daughter, I ask you to keep these five stones and a burnt stick in the utmost safety of your heart. For it is you who—until the chosen one bears in her womb the Son of God—must teach, share, celebrate and live the truth of these symbols. It is you who with

EPILOGUE

wisdom will share their meaning with all other women, and with all those open to their truth."

Miriam wept as she read her father's message and then, turning to look once more upon his face, carefully replaced the lambskin in its hessian bag. She had much to ponder, but in the beauty of this sacred moment she paused to hear the silent music of this tent of meeting and to see the glory that such intimacy conveys. And then she rose, resolved to go and tell the others.

Acknowledgments

So many people have influenced this book that it would be impossible to mention them all. But I must say special thanks to my beloved wife Marie for her support; my wonderful mama Britzaida and papa JM Ernesto, now writing stories in the clouds; my sisters Glo, Patty, and Becky; my family; all my faithful friends from all times and places; the Ark T Centre; the James Street community; the people of St. Luke's Oxford, Henley and Remenham; Rev. Rosemary Ashley who encouraged me to do something with the original idea; Abbi Strevens for helping with the first drafts; and most of all, to Clare Allsop for all her assistance with the final text and finally to my dear friend, Jan Spurlock Stockland, who took the text to a different level. Thank you.

About The Author

Ernesto Lozada-Uzuriaga Steele is a Peruvian writer and painter currently living in the south of England. He studied Theology and Social Anthropology in Lima and trained for the ministry at Wycliffe Hall, Oxford. He is a co-founder of the Ark T Centre, Oxford, and a founder member of The Creative Tent of Makers & Keepers. Ernesto divides his time between creative endeavors and serving his community as an Anglican minister.

www.whisperingtreeoriginalbooks.com

www.ingramcontent.com/pod-product-compliance
Lightning Source LLC
Chambersburg PA
CBHW051707040426
42446CB00008B/759